ASPATORE
C-Level Business Intelligence™

Praise for Books, Business Intelligence Publications & Services

"What C-Level executives read to keep their edge and make pivotal business decisions. Timeless classics for indispensable knowledge." - Richard Costello, Manager-Corporate Marketing Communication, General Electric (NYSE: GE)

"True insight from the doers in the industry, as opposed to the critics on the sideline." - Steve Hanson, CEO, On Semiconductor (NASDAQ: ONNN)

"Unlike any other business books, Inside the Minds captures the essence, the deep-down thinking processes, of people who make things happen." - Martin Cooper, CEO, Arraycomm

"The only useful way to get so many good minds speaking on a complex topic." - Scott Bradner, Senior Technical Consultant, Harvard University

"What the bigwigs read." - Paul Simons, CEO, Ogilvy & Mather UK

"An important read for those who want to gain insight....lifetimes of knowledge and understanding..." - Anthony Russo, Ph.D., CEO, Noonan Russo Communications

"A tremendous treasure trove of knowledge...perfect for the novice or the seasoned veteran."- Thomas L. Amberg, CEO, Cushman Amberg Communications

"A unique and startling look..." - Lee Duffey, President, Duffey Communications

ASPATORE
C-Level Business Intelligence™

Publisher of Books, Business Intelligence Publications & Services
www.Aspatore.com

Aspatore is the world's largest and most exclusive publisher of C-Level executives (CEO, CFO, CTO, CMO, Partner) from the world's most respected companies. Aspatore annually publishes C-Level executives from over half the Global 500, top 250 professional services firms, law firms (MPs/Chairs), and other leading companies of all sizes in books, briefs, reports, articles and other publications. By focusing on publishing only C-Level executives, Aspatore provides professionals of all levels with proven business intelligence from industry insiders, rather than relying on the knowledge of unknown authors and analysts. Aspatore publishes an innovative line of business intelligence resources including Inside the Minds, Bigwig Briefs, ExecRecs, Business Travel Bible, Brainstormers, The C-Level Test, and Aspatore Business Journals, in addition to other best selling business books, briefs and essays. Aspatore also provides an array of business services including The C-Level Library, PIA Reports, SmartPacks, and The C-Level Review, as well as outsourced business library and researching capabilities. Aspatore focuses on traditional print publishing and providing business intelligence services, while our portfolio companies, Corporate Publishing Group (B2B writing & editing), Aspatore Speaker's Network, and Aspatore Stores focus on developing areas within the business and publishing worlds.

INSIDE THE MINDS:
Leading Women

What it Takes For Women to Succeed and Have it All in the 21st Century

ASPATORE
C-Level Business Intelligence™

Published by Aspatore, Inc.
For information on bulk orders, sponsorship opportunities or any other questions please email sales@aspatore.com. For corrections, company/title updates, comments or any other inquiries please email info@aspatore.com.

Third Printing, February 2003
10 9 8 7 6 5 4 3 2 1

ISBN 1-58762-019-7

Library of Congress Card Number: 2001086980

Cover design by Michael Lepera/Ariosto Graphics & James Weinberg

Material in this book is for educational purposes only. This book is sold with the understanding that neither any of the interviewees or the publisher is engaged in rendering legal, accounting, investment, or any other professional service.

This book is printed on acid free paper.

A special thanks to all the individuals that made this book possible:

Jennifer Openshaw, Tiffany Bass Bukow, Patricia Dunn, Vivian Banta, Kerri Lee Sinclair, Kim Fischer, Krishna Subramanian, Mona Lisa Wallace, Emily Hofstetter and Lisa Henderson

Special thanks also to: Brigeth Rivera, Ted Juliano, Kirsten Catanzano, Susan Chernauskas, and Melissa Conradi

The views expressed by the individuals in this book do not necessarily reflect the views shared by the companies they are employed by (or the companies mentioned in this book). The companies referenced may not be the same company that the individual works for since the publishing of this book.

**Please note that all Inside the Minds books published since this book originally appeared in 2001 do not appear in an interview style, but rather a normal essay format.

Inside the Minds:
Leading Women

What it Takes For Women to Succeed and Have it All in the 21st Century

Contents

INSIDE THE MINDS

Empowering Professionals of All Levels
With C-Level Business Intelligence
www.InsideTheMinds.com

The critically acclaimed *Inside the Minds* series provides readers of all levels with proven business intelligence from C-Level executives (CEO, CFO, CTO, CMO, Partner) from the world's most respected companies. Each chapter is comparable to a white paper or essay and is a future-oriented look at where an industry/profession/topic is heading and the most important issues for future success. Each author has been carefully chosen through an exhaustive selection process by the *Inside the Minds* editorial board to write a chapter for this book. *Inside the Minds* was conceived in order to give readers actual insights into the leading minds of business executives worldwide. Because so few books or other publications are actually written by executives in industry, *Inside the Minds* presents an unprecedented look at various industries and professions never before available.

For information on bulk orders, sponsorship opportunities or any other questions, please email store@aspatore.com.

For information on licensing the content in this book, or any content published by Aspatore, please email jonp@aspatore.com.

To nominate yourself, another individual, or a group of executives for an upcoming Inside the Minds book, or to suggest a specific topic for an Inside the Minds book, please email jason@aspatore.com.

JENNIFER OPENSHAW
Setting and Achieving Goals
Women's Financial Network
Founder

Tell me what you enjoy most about what you're doing today.

There's nothing better than creating a vision and then assembling a team of people who believe in it to make it a reality. I can recall days where we'd get phone calls from people who would see us on CNBC and want to work for us because we were doing something new and unique in an area for which many people had a deep passion. To me, everyday is about working to make the vision bigger and better and keeping high enthusiasm among the troops in good markets and bad. I personally compare a company to a living organism - a network of complex organs and systems integrated and dependent on each other. As the person running the company, I have to assume the role of the central nervous system, monitoring all aspects of the company and making sure everything is working properly and in harmony.

I love a challenge - constant challenges that teach me new things and take me to new places. I'm not someone who can remain idle so I get a constant renewal from engaging in a variety of areas - from the staff to investors to board members to the public. Every single day there's something new coming in - from significant competitors to a new technology to consider. I enjoy dealing with that every day, not knowing what each day is going to bring.

Making a difference in people's lives also gives meaning to my vision. When I come home at 10:00 PM at night and open up my email and find over a hundred emails from people who appreciate what I've done for them - telling me how I've inspired them to take the next step toward whatever dreams they want to fulfill - that makes the tough times worth it.

Why did you choose to go into women's finances?

That decision was as much personal as it was professional. My mother divorced when I was 5 and left with three very young children. She was not formally educated, so she had to figure out how to support these three kids. She ultimately took two full-time jobs as a waitress, working from 9:00 AM to 4:00 PM and then again from 6:00 PM to 12:00 AM, obviously placing a tremendous

7

burden on her. As I learned more about my what my mother had to go through I realized that women's financial needs differ from men's because of issues like death and divorce, which leave women more likely to have their financial resources depleted. As the primary caretaker of their family, women must also think of long-term care and how it will be paid for. Women are working today in dual income households, making it nearly impossible to stay home with aging parents, as we used to in days past. The bottom line is that women today live longer yet they earn less, save less, and are far more likely to face poverty than men - so they must do better with their finances. Yet, many women lack the knowledge or confidence to get started.

I ultimately saw an opportunity to create a company that differed from all of the news or information only sites as well as the financial services sites - a company that combined both aspects and dealt with financial matters in a way that women could relate to. Nearly every financial institution has a program to specifically target women, but I felt it could be done more successfully from a business standpoint. My work as the on-camera financial commentator for CBS-TV in Los Angeles confirmed my instincts, as women would write sharing their fears and concerns. It was further validated when I met with CEOs and other top executives from across the country, who wondered about many of the same issues. How do you talk to your parents about their finances? When do you take them over? Do you create joint accounts with your husband? What happens in the event of divorce? How do I protect what I have? It goes on and on.

What do you think is causing the increase in affluent women, or women who are generating more wealth?

From 1996-1998, the number of affluent women increased 69% to 14.8 million while the number of affluent men increased just 36% to 14.3 million. The primary factor driving this is sheer hard work. One study found that women got their wealth not through inheritances, but through their own efforts in the workforce. And, women are working largely because of a need for dual incomes while others are starting businesses (at twice the rate as men) to create their own opportunities. Women are moving up the career ladder, and they're doing it a bit faster for two reasons: 1) they're more educated than ever before, seeking MBAs or technical degrees and 2) they are successful managers.

Are there certain hurdles that women moving up the corporate ladder are not facing as much now as they might have a couple of years ago?

The corporate community has started to realize the value of leaders that have a strong "EQ," or "emotional quotient" in addition to more traditional skills. A company's human assets are not only their most important assets, they're their most expensive. So, skills that make good use of these assets are absolutely critical. Women tend to differ from men, studies show, in that they are more intuitive, more inclusive, more nurturing, more communicative, and place a higher value on consensus building, bringing in other team members into the process, for instance. As more and more companies and recruiters recognize this, they'll be looking for people with high EQs, and that oftentimes happens to be women.

The fact that women today make or influence 80% of their family's financial decisions, buy 50% of cars and electronics, and are the primary health care decision makers tells us that they are driving purchases. This can have a circular affect in leading companies to put women in positions focused on marketing or understanding the customer. I serve on the advisory board of Wyndham Hotels. They're an excellent example of a company that understands that women will drive the future growth of their company.

Acknowledgement by both the media and the general public is key to moving up the corporate ladder. This didn't happen so much in the past because women weren't seen as leaders but as the support staff. Today, while progress still needs to be made here, we're hearing more and more about the success of the female manager. That gets attention, which means she's in demand, which drives up her value and the opportunities she can pursue.

Finally, the opportunities that have opened up for women are in an entirely different league from those in the past. The fact that the economy has shifted from an industrial foundation reliant upon physical processes to a services and information economy reliant on intellectual assets opened up more opportunities for women. Women are quickly moving into positions traditionally held by men - such as engineers, CTOs, scientists, COOs and even in finance. These are generally higher paying positions than the jobs traditionally held by women in human resources, communications, and administration, for instance.

Tell me about some of the roadblocks you've encountered over the course of your career, up to WFN.

I come from a singe parent household at a very young age in which just paying the bills were tough. My mother wasn't formally educated and I didn't really have any guidance. So I figured that if I wanted to make something of myself and of my life, I was going to have to figure it out for myself. As early as eight years old, I remember making napkin ring holders to sell as Christmas gifts. At age 14 I took a job as a maid in a low-scale motel. I took a more serious attitude about my life than probably most kids that age, developing my own vision of doing something significant in this world.

Capital raising as a woman isn't easy either. In fact, only about 4% of venture capital goes to women. Sure, that's in part due to the fact that women haven't always pursued it - because they didn't understand it. How do you break into the venture capital world, which is a close-knit community - a bit of an insiders club? That closeness is partly understandable: as an investor, you want to put your money with people you know and trust, people with a solid track record. But how can you develop a track record if not given the chance? It becomes a chicken and the egg question. As a female, I was able to break down a lot of barriers and build a successful company - and do it in the private equity mostly male world of Silicon Valley. I believe I was able to do that because I had a strong business model, passion, and worked with a few people - men and women - who helped mentor me.

Finally, I uprooted myself - took the risk to go off entirely on my own - to pursue my vision (my investor was in the Bay Area and I was in LA). I had to make the decision to enter into a completely new environment, without any type of support structure, without any contacts, without any friends, and just believe in what I was doing. It was not easy and, frankly, I have sacrificed a lot as I've worked to pursue my vision - time with family and others who were very important to me.

What gives you your tenacity?

First and foremost, there's a feeling that never goes away that there's always something to be done - or that something can be done better. I wouldn't necessarily call myself a perfectionist but I don't accept that things can't be done. I'm a big believer that if there's a will there's a way. And, if I am working on a vision or a goal and an opportunity presents itself that furthers that vision or goal, I almost never say no. The downside is that one can take on too much. The goal is to capitalize on the opportunities while ensuring you're still doing a good job.

I would also say vision. I had created this vision at the ripe old age of 12 that I would do something that combined the greater good with my interest in the media and business. Whether I was working out or working as a waitress, I'd recall my vision, which would keep me moving toward the next goal, the next rung in climbing the ladder.

I also get enormous satisfaction from getting things done. It gives me a sense of accomplishment. I'm a list person, checking off each item as it's accomplished. But I also think beyond - what can I do to further the vision, to make the company better? Then, I develop my strategy and go after it.

What's your "sales" strategy, whether you're raising money for your company, trying to get through school, or getting to the next level of where you want to be?

Getting others to buy into your dream or vision and getting them to realize the value that's in it for them. The question you must ask yourself in any sales strategy is, "How are you going to enter into a mutually rewarding partnership?" It's the recognition that successful endeavors are not zero sum games. It's really the understanding that an arrangement can be made that's a win-win for both parties. I remember when I was at Wilshire Associates, one of the largest institutional investment consulting firms in the country and producer of the Wilshire 5000 Total Market Index. The company had a stellar reputation in the financial community and wanted to expand their name recognition. They had tremendous assets, one of which was the Wilshire 5000 Index. I decided that my ultimate goal was to get CNBC to use the index regularly - after all, it is considered by Wall Street experts to be the best measure of the entire US stock market. My strategy was to give CNBC an exclusive right to use the index. So CNBC obtained rights to the best financial information and Wilshire achieved their goal of increased brand awareness. It was a win-win.

You talked a little bit about goals. How important has setting goals been through the course of your career, and how have they changed?

Setting goals is an absolutely key part of my life, on a daily basis, a weekly basis, and a long-term basis. I set a goal when I was age 12 and I haven't stopped. Every year I set my goals for the coming year with a close friend. I think about what I need to do over the course of the year to reach that goal. And

11

then I set goals quarterly and weekly - goals that the entire organization is working toward. Where possible, I implement monitoring systems so that everyone can see what the goals are or how they stack up in the market. Goals are really essential to aligning the interests of the entire organization. On a personal level, they help keep you focused. They help you determine where you should spend your time, and where you shouldn't. It can make decisions much easier. The goals become your roadmap.

When I go through a career change, I always consider what the goals are of any next move - what is it that I want to accomplish? What's important to me? How does it fit in with my skills and interests? Will it take me to where I might want to go next?

Today, my goals incorporate more personal development than they might have five or ten years ago.

You find a lot of people get stuck in a rut. They're comfortable. How would you advise another person if a risk is worth taking?

You must first determine if you can withstand the worst-case scenario. If you start a company, for instance, will you be all right if it fails? You must determine if you have enough confidence in your ability and tenacity to survive the worst-case scenario. This is also a time in which gut instinct comes into play. Ultimately, we can never be 100% certain about a decision - but does it feel right? Are you getting indications or are the doors opening such that you're receiving confirmation that this is a direction that perhaps makes sense?

The worst-case scenario might even mean that you're out of a job, so do you have the skills and relationships or savings to be able to take care of yourself? To me that's a familiar example of a worst-case scenario. Does it help you to reach your goal, does it capitalize on some of the assets you have, and do you feel passionate about it? You can have some skills, but if you don't feel passionate about taking that risk - starting a new company or running a new company - it won't work. You need to have both the skills and the passion. It's not just about the skills that you've built in the past. What's your passion and what do you want to do next? What excites you, what interests you? How do you not get overloaded with everything going on?

I'm known for overloading myself but I try to keep it in control by creating to-do lists for the day and week. While driving into work, I'll write down what I hope to accomplish for the day. It's usually a lot, so to get it done I delegate and I multi-task. For example, if I'm on hold on the phone, I'm checking email or reviewing something with an employee. Finally, I just keep moving forward and thinking about the goal. The rush of doing many things gives me more energy.

How have you been able to balance your business and personal life?

It's not easy but I try to compartmentalize. So that when I'm allowing myself free time, personal time, I try not to bring my laptop with me. I also tell myself that if I accomplish what I hope on the job, then I deserve a little reward. That reward could be a two-hour walk, a massage, or a movie. For me, exercise brings balance to my life, though it takes a bit of time, but it reduces stress and makes me function at a higher capacity. Finally, I've learned that the people who provide emotional support to you are critical to your business life. That by having a strong support system at home you can function better on the job. So, investing time and attention to the personal side is critical.

You obviously do things outside of work. What's the balance you need to be most efficient? What gives you the fuel?

Success gives me fuel. Each success gives me validation and energy to go to the next step. But I believe the best balance is to devote time to the personal side of life, which really is the support system for the business side of life. It's circular; one feeds off the other. I am finally at a point where I believe I have earned the right to focus more on my personal priorities, that I don't have to work 18 hour days, 7 days a week. I firmly believe that taking that time will not only help me achieve balance in my life, but better prepare me for the next professional challenge.

How important has networking been for you?

I don't like the term networking. The fact is you meet people day in and day out. You may meet a phenomenal person in whom your interests coincide or there appears to be a natural opportunity to work together for that win-win. So, I like to suggest that people simply keep themselves open to the possibilities - and to stay interested in the needs of the other person. If you can do that, and that is often difficult in this day and age, you will see more opportunities come back than you ever imagined.

Many people venture into a new area in which they don't have a network. When I raised seed financing for WFN, I barely knew a single person in the venture capital world. It was the passion for the business that ultimately led me to succeed.

There's a certain amount of genuineness. When people deal with you and get a good sense that you're not trying to spin a line or push a product, but that you are dealing with them in a straightforward manner, they will tend to want to align with you. Value everyone you meet because the relationships you build early on will be with you for the rest of your life and you never know when you're interests might coincide.

Tell me some qualities that you admire.

I expect people to do what they say they're going to do. I was especially impressed when HP's Carly Fiorina turned down her executive bonus because the company had not met its performance goals. Rarely is that done in the business world. That kind of action inspires more confidence in and respect for the leader.

Risking your reputation is not an easy thing to do, but it's something I admire when someone believes in something so strongly that they take the risk. It might be a new idea or a strategy for handling a crisis that isn't generally supported.

Today, so many people are focused on themselves and forget the larger picture. I respect people who can put their ego aside and put the interests of the greater good first. That also means surrounding themselves with the highest quality professionals, as opposed to "yes-men."

There's just no substitute for honesty and hard work. If you're working with the right people, honesty and hard work can take you far. I remember a talented CFO in Silicon Valley who underscored my honesty - that trait told him a lot about me and what he could expect when times get tough or things don't go as one would hope.

Tell me about your managerial style.

I hold people accountable, starting first and foremost with myself. But I also believe you need to give people the support and tools to be accountable. The Air Force uses the terms "centralized control" and "decentralized execution." The generals choose the strategy and the goals, but once you have to go out to execute, you have to trust that the people who are skilled, trained, and closer to the issue are in a better position to execute.

Mistakes are part of learning. I believe in allowing people to make mistakes so long as they learn from them. I've certainly made mistakes but each time I do I try take whatever action I can to correct it, to prevent it from happening again.

Getting employees to maintain their enthusiasm means showing appreciation. The impact of a few dollars spent on food, for instance, comes back 10 fold in more output and positive feelings about the company. I want my employees to believe in the product so much that it pervades everything they do, when they come into contact with vendors, partners, the public and with the media, because that excitement exudes and it helps the company go to the next step. People like to be recognized for their work, so I try to do it in public. That has the double effect of rewarding the person and telling others that their work will not go unnoticed. It goes back to praise in public, criticize in private.

Lead by example. That means if you want people working long hours, come in early and let them see what it takes. And that also means if you're going to chat on the phone, suggest to other people they can do that.

Holding people accountable. I think it's really important to be clear about what you expect of other people. Certainly some of this is learned the hard way. Really taking time to listen to people, because it's so easy when you're moving very quickly not to listen. It's also important as a manager to take time away to reflect and think and sometimes come up with magical ideas that can propel the business. I like people to run with the ball. I think having ownership of a project or an area is key. I think it's important to remember that doing little things for an employee, like bringing in food, or I even took all my employees to a spa for the day. The cost of that is minuscule when you think about how much that comes back to you. You're making people feel like they've received something and are appreciated, encouraging them to work even longer. If managers did a little bit more of that they would see even more come back.

How important is it to keep learning and pushing yourself in new directions, to take your skills to the next level? Where should people be learning - team building, technical knowledge?

There's no finish line in the race to perfection. You realize you never know everything you need to know. And, in fact, as you get older you learn that you know far less than you ever thought. The challenge of understanding ourselves, at least for me, becomes greater. The process of understanding yourself personally and developing yourself professionally, if those are your goals, is a lifelong process. People should be constantly endeavoring to renew themselves in terms of understanding society, how people get along, what affects people. It's important to understand that self-actualization is beyond what we just learn in school, but what we learn in everyday life. The more you understand yourself, the more effective you can be in dealing with other people despite all the technology and the Internet. It affects how we communicate and how we accept other people's ideas and how we negotiate - and how, ultimately, you'll succeed as a top manager. I think it's important to understand other industries and their impact on your business. I like to push people to think a step beyond what they might normally. So while they might follow what's going on in their industry, there might be another industry where an incredible partnership could be struck if you just thought outside the box.

What does it take to become a leader?

That all depends. There are different kinds of leaders. Transactional leaders can come in and take over a company, much like a COO. There's nothing really cathartic going on, though they can lead teams of people. That's certainly different from a visionary who attempts to create a vision of something that's never been achieved before but who may need to rely on the transactional leader to execute on the vision. And then there are transformational leaders like Abraham Lincoln and Jack Welch who can break something down only to rebuild it better and stronger than it was before.

A leader is someone who can turn weaknesses into strengths. A leader is someone who can find value in every opportunity, even in the people who may not seem very skilled or talented. A successful leader can coach these people and get them to bring real value to the organization.

A leader is also willing to take risks, and he or she knows how to do it. She is constantly willing to put herself in new situations, to take on the challenge. A leader sees this as an opportunity to grow with the experience, even if there are failures.

A leader can chart a company not only through good times but also in bad. Muscling the troops, igniting passion, getting them to commit even during a tough challenge, and working toward the goal.

Jennifer Openshaw is Founder and Vice Chair of WFN, and served as the Company's Chairman, President and CEO prior to its acquisition by Siebert Financial. Ms. Openshaw built WFN into the Internet's leading financial company designed to help women build and manage their wealth. The site has been hailed as one of the sites to bookmark by several national publications, including Business Week, Kiplinger's Personal Finance and the Chicago Tribune. Ms. Openshaw was recently named one of the Internet's 25 Rising Stars by Internet World magazine.

Before launching WFN, Ms. Openshaw served as Director of Investment Services for Wilshire Associates, one of the nation's largest investment consulting firms and producer of the Wilshire 5000 Total Market Index. Prior to joining Wilshire, Ms. Openshaw served as a Vice President in the Investment Management Services Group at Bank of America. She was also Press Secretary to California State Treasurer Kathleen Brown, where she was involved in launching several small business lending programs and creating California's "Save at School" program designed to teach kids about finance.

A former Rotary Scholar in Australia, Ms. Openshaw holds an MBA and BA from UCLA. She also serves on the Advisory Board of Wyndham Hotels and is a member of Young Entrepreneurs' Organization.

TIFFANY BASS BUKOW
The Path to Success
MsMoney
Founder & CEO

How did you become a Dot.com CEO?

It took fifteen years, a lot of tenacity, flexibility, optimism and vision. I would have to say though that my job experiences over those years aligned quite nicely to prepare me to take advantage of many opportunities, which ultimately led to my dream job as a CEO.

I have had many people in my life say that I have been lucky and sometimes I certainly feel that way. However, I have spent a lifetime preparing myself to take advantage of this luck!

It all started in 1983 in High school in Chicago where I took my first computer-programming course, and I fell in love with the technology. Before computers, I had always been interested in the mechanics behind tape recorders and televisions and wanted to know how they worked. I used to fantasize when I was five years old about watching a television that would be just a little bigger than the size of a watch. Ten years later that technology became a reality.

At age 16, I was introduced to this complex piece of machinery called a computer and it gave me a whole new sense of awe. I could not have imagined at the time how this magic box with its lines of code and punch cards would change the way the world did business when I grew up. I did however have the vision at that early age that it was something I should learn more about.

When I attended college, I enrolled as a computer engineer. I soon realized that my interests were more focused on the business aspects of computer applications instead of building the underlying technology. I changed my direction and studied Management Information Systems and Marketing.

My favorite class was a Management and Business Analysis class that used Harvard Business School Case Studies as the foundation of teaching. We broke out into work teams and analyzed the data for days until the professor would randomly choose one student to present to the class. Our task was to act as the

19

CEO of the company we were analyzing and to set forth the strategic plan of action the company should take to be successful. We would pretend that we were talking to our Board of Directors (something I would learn a lot about much later). The professor, after our speech, would let us know what the best course of action really was and what the company actually did in real life. I received one of the highest grades in the class and learned that I was a good strategic thinker and not afraid to share my views in public. It was then I started to realize that I wanted to be a CEO of my own company some day.

I was 20 years old and had no idea how I would do this, after all I didn't know any CEO's or even any high level executives. I came from a working class town and was pretty naïve about the ways of the corporate world. (The mistakes I made my first year in the corporate world were pretty humorous - but that is whole another story). I did keep the goal of becoming a CEO in the back of my mind for the next ten years until it became a reality.

After college I had wanted to go work for a big consulting firm (which is what a lot my friends and MIS majors did). Unfortunately (or maybe fortunately looking back now) it did not work out. So instead, I landed a job in marketing where I worked for a few years supporting worldwide brands. One of the first people I befriended, at the new multi-billion dollar company I worked, was the CEO. My bosses and cohorts thought I was nuts to be socializing with the head guy, but I didn't know any better. He was just another person to me. Looking back now it seemed like I had planned it, even though I didn't know what I was doing at the time. The knowledge and experience I picked up in the marketing world would be critical in the B2C (business to consumer) branding phase I was to enter ten years later with my own company.

At 23 years old, after working as a Marketing Assistant for two years, I decided I was working much too hard and making way too little money. So after observing numerous Sales Representatives driving around in their expensive sports cars and designer suits, I decided there has got to be a better way for me to develop my career. So I joined their ranks and spent some time working as a Sales Representative for a Fortune 500 technology company.

My life changed overnight.

I became the number one Sales Rep in my district and closed two of the biggest deals the sales branch had ever seen. I was now working half the hours I used at my old job and was making twice the amount of money. Life was good! The formal training I received in sales would be invaluable as I took on the role of business development for my own company many years later.

20

After another two years, I decided it was time to look for new challenges, so I headed back to graduate school to refresh my computer skills and to study multimedia and instructional design. After all, computers were my first love. I didn't know in 1993, when I enrolled, that the Internet I would use for research for my Master Degree would become the foundation of the New Economy.

Before I grappled with the New Economy, I wanted to learn something about the Global Economy. I took the summer off between Grad school years and backpacked alone through Europe. This was quite an accomplishment for me to travel by myself. I had never been outside the country, nor had I ever traveled alone. I conquered the fear of the unknown and bought a roundtrip ticket to Paris.

When you travel by yourself you get a lot more done, so I managed to see twenty cities and ten countries in just two months. I used the solitary time for introspection and to seek a fuller understanding of the world. It was a real eye-opening experience and I was exposed to situations and cultures that are indelibly marked in my memory. I couldn't have known at the time that just four years later I would take a full year off on my honeymoon and see ten times as much of the world and even speak at the first Internet World conference in India. I also didn't know that in 6 years I would begin my quest to create a global financial literacy program to help eliminate the poverty I had seen on my travels by teaching the world the fundamentals of saving for future goals.

My timing for Grad school was perfect and I was uniquely prepared to capitalize on the Multimedia Revolution. During my last semester in 1995 I participated as an intern at a Multimedia startup that made CD-ROM games. I was surprised at the chaotic nature of the environment. It was thirty people in one big dusty warehouse south of market in San Francisco with no walls and no rules. Quite a change from the structured corporate environments I came from where I was required to wear skirts and high heels and our manner of conduct was dictated. This multimedia startup managed to raise a few million dollars and began to put their plans in motion. I didn't know at that time I would also have my own few million dollars and twenty people in a warehouse south of market in San Francisco just four years later.

Shortly after the internship ended, and sadly unable to find a job in CD-ROM production, I decided to volunteer my time to help my school develop the first online multimedia educational course. We used Netscape 1.0 as our development browser. This was before Microsoft even thought the Internet was a viable business opportunity. How could I have known that in just five years later that my own company would win a multimillion-dollar contract to create online educational programs for one of the biggest banks in the world and we would be responsible for teaching millions of Americans about personal finance?

After I finished the development of this first Internet course, I decided it was time to bring in some income. I was introduced to a partner who had an idea to create a financial services site that focused on education instead of just financial products. This was quite novel at the time since no one was doing this. Most Web sites were "brochureware" and had little educational quality or even interactivity.

I was excited to be doing something that would have social impact and still be a very lucrative and profitable business. A gal still has to make a living (after all I didn't inherit any wealth), so even though I was a philanthropist at heart, I had my eye on business and making money. At my new startup, I spent my time hiring a production team, creating prototypes, writing a business plan and speaking to many advisors. But alas, it was early 1996 and the Dot.com craze had not quite taken off yet and I started to realize it wasn't that easy to raise money, especially as a female 28 year old asking for five million dollars from strangers. After six months working for a paltry pay, funded by my partner, and an enormous number of eventually worthless stock options, I was forced to make a change.

I decided to head out on my own path and see what fate brought in. It was probably the worst time in my life to do this since I had just separated from a long-term relationship and had no where to live, had no money, my car had just gotten stolen and I had two ruptured disks in my neck. But I guess I really didn't have a choice. The job offers weren't flowing in and I needed to do something.

What I did do, even though I just left the financial services startup, was not completely abandon the idea of a financial services site. Fundamentally I knew that the Internet would be a terrific place to offer financial education online and the public would begin demanding it. But instead of trying to compete with huge players like Quicken who might decide to enter the general market, I decided to find my own little niche.

That niche was women. I acquired the domain name MsMoney.com and began planning a company that focused on educating women how to take financial control of their lives. I was a woman who had overcome great odds to get where I was today and the reason I was surviving in the midst of turmoil and still fearless was because I had taken financial control of my life. I wanted to share my knowledge with the rest of the world and let them know anyone could do it because it wasn't that hard once you knew how.

Unfortunately it was 1996 and only 18% of the Internet consisted of women. So it was not quite the time to start this new venture. So instead of embarking on the MsMoney.com plan, I had to create a Plan B. I spent time evaluating my skills and my resources and decided that opening my own Internet Consulting practice would be a good idea. I had a barbecue and invited all my friends over to announce to them that I was officially opening my office doors (which led to my dining room) as an Internet Consultant. My company name would be Tiff.Com and I would later become more affectionately known by my friends as Tiff Dot Com instead of Tiffany Bass.

The business started slowly and it was scary at first since I didn't really have any capital to start the business. Not only that, I had quite a few student loans and no income coming in. But I decided that going out on my own was worth the risk. I laid out all my credit cards on the table and added up my credit amount. I decided I would give the new business a year using my 10 credit cards as capital. It was pretty easy to get the high interest rate pre-approved credit cards in the mail, but very hard to get a real business loan from the bank.

The great thing was, I didn't even need to use this credit line. I was instantly profitable with my first account. Ok - so it wasn't very hard to be profitable, since all I had was an old used Mac, a printer, a scanner, a phone and a dining room for an office. I was happy and my newly hatched plan was working. Whew!

In just two short years I went from a one person Internet Consulting and Web Design Shop to a twenty-person company with Fortune 100 clients such as Sun, AOL, Bechtel, and Lucent. I was helping these Industry Leaders design and launch their websites. I felt pretty cool!

I started getting job offers from larger design firms who wanted me to come in and run their Internet consulting divisions. These are the same type of companies who turned me down in college. I figured, why would I want to go work for them now? Once you create your own culture and rules it is incredibly hard to go back to someone else's and survive let alone thrive.

In 1999, I attended the Internet World in LA and was pleased by what was happening in the Financial Services world on the Internet. People were really starting to use the Internet to educate themselves about money and they were even buying financial products online. I had been correct in predicting this trend. I had also been right that women would start flocking to the Net in droves. In 1999 women made up 50% of the online traffic. I was ready for my new plan.

This was the information that propelled me to officially start dedicating my energy to building the MsMoney.com website. It was the peak of the Dot.com era and I wasn't going to miss out by building everyone else's dream and being a consultant. I wanted to create something of my own. I wanted to impact the world and create social change by helping women become financially empowered.

I was in a unique position to start MsMoney because of the Tiff.com business. The core Tiff.Com team built the original prototype of MsMoney.com. I used the prototype to secure partnerships and generate interest amongst investors. Once I raised money, I converted the Tiff.Com team to MsMoney employees and handed out those coveted stock options.

My life was about to enter a whirlwind. No - let me rephrase that - it was about to enter a hurricane! My new motto became, "What doesn't kill me only makes me stronger!" I faced every conceivable challenge you could imagine as a new CEO. We had technology problems, office space problems, phone problems, employee problems that led to firings and lawsuit threats. We had to get out of bad contracts, cope with losing key personnel, compete with 6 new competitors, overcome the fallout of the market, deal with investors who turned us down, realize our business plan was not viable, and eventually change our strategy. We had to hire new teams for the new vision, secure clients who could pay the bills, try to reduce our bills and the list goes on. It had been by far the most grueling year of my life. But because of that, it was also the most rewarding.

Describe an obstacle you have overcome on the way to making your business a success?

In Fall of 1999 MsMoney was riding high on the success of Dot.com Mania. It seemed as if there wasn't anything MsMoney couldn't conquer. I had received a commitment of three million dollars in financing in December of 1999, which gave my company a twenty million dollar valuation. We began to ramp up production immediately and run down the IPO path. I was fairly confident that I could raise another twenty million in the summer for a marketing campaign to let the world know that we were here to help secure women's financial future. It wouldn't be long before we went public and raised hundreds of millions of dollars. MsMoney grew from a handful of people to fifteen full time employees in just a few months. And on March 29, 2000 we launched the MsMoney.com website with the participation of the First Lady Hillary Rodham Clinton. Her presence made a world of difference. Yahoo's television cameras were at our offices memorializing our launch event and an entrepreneur roundtable with the First Lady. It was all being broadcasted via satellite across the entire country.

We celebrated at our launch party with six hundred people in the Grand Ballroom at the swanky Hotel W in downtown San Francisco.

In just thirty days, we went from a virtually unknown company to a household name. USA Today and Yahoo! named us the Hot Site of the Week. We had over 40 positive press mentions in the following months, including The Wall Street Journal, Fortune, ABC News, PBS, Forbes, Business 2.0, Time, Working Woman and The Industry Standard.

It all appeared to be a rosy picture and our future seemed secure. The market was HOT! We had six competitors appear shortly after us. Everyone wanted to be in the financial services business targeting women.

But then in April the Stock Market crashed...And my life dramatically changed again!

It seemed as if Dot.com's had fallen out of favor overnight. The dreams of thousands of entrepreneurs went up in smoke and hundreds of millions of investor's dollars went down the drain.

It didn't help soothe my thoughts that I wasn't the only one who spent millions of dollars chasing an unrealistic dream that the world would stop everything they were doing and use the Internet for everything in their lives.

I had to ask myself - Why had I fallen prey to the frenzy of the Internet? Why had I put solid business acumen on the backburner in favor of the latest trend? It wasn't as if I was new to the online world. MsMoney was my third Internet company since 1995. I had run a profitable and successful Dot.com before (Tiff.com). I even held the MsMoney.com name for three years before I created a business around it so that I could wait for the right timing.

But the timing wasn't right, not just for me, but for the thousands of other Dot.com's who thought they were going to change the world overnight.

Now I was faced with a real challenge: MsMoney had spent over two million dollars in six months and was in need of an additional cash infusion. The three million dollar commitment I received the previous December only materialized into two million dollar after the market crash. I couldn't in good conscious take another million from investors when I knew that it was unlikely MsMoney could be a profitable business any time soon.

So what was I to do? We were out of money. The disappointment I felt was enormous. Twenty people relied on me for their livelihood and investors had given me millions of dollars in the hopes of a profitable outcome.

I had no choice but to pick up the pieces of dashed hopes and broken dreams and start treading down a new path. I would not accept failure as part of my resume. I put on the happiest face I could muster and summoned my optimistic old self who had been buried in the rubble of the Internet fall-out and began to inspire the MsMoney troops.

Not everyone could understand my newfound cheerfulness. Some of the MsMoney team couldn't overcome the uncertainty and the fear of failing and left for safer and more stable ground immediately.

I too wanted to be on safer ground and quickly devised a plan to get us there. I had run a profitable Internet company before and new I could do it again. In this case, I had to do it again very quickly or MsMoney would go bankrupt.

In just sixty days I re-positioned MsMoney from a financial services website designed to help women secure their financial future to a financial services Internet Consulting company which helped Financial Institutions build their websites and reach targeted consumers. In that short time, I convinced one of the industry leaders in online banking to let MsMoney help them redesign their website and develop customized content for their consumers.

Overnight, we became profitable and it looked like MsMoney was going to survive.

But that wasn't the end of the story. Not everyone in the company wanted MsMoney JUST to survive. Some folks came on board wanting MsMoney to IPO - to go public - so that they could cash in their dreams and retire millionaires in just a couple years. When the cash dream faded, their enthusiasm for MsMoney faded. They didn't want to just work at a company that was only profitable, they wanted to hit it big! So ultimately I ended up losing some of the higher-level executives because there wasn't enough financial reward to attract them to stay.

In the end though, I feel that MsMoney is a better company because of the turmoil that we went through. The core team that stayed through the difficulties feels very bonded to each other and committed to MsMoney's long-term goals of changing the way consumers learn about managing their money and securing their financial future. They are very passionate about their work and truly believe that they can make a difference in the world. Though they may not retire millionaires next year, they feel that the work they are doing is far more rewarding. This is the type of people I want supporting the MsMoney mission.

What advice would you give a startup?

Startups are faced with challenges that most established companies are not. There is a whole additional set of rules for this industry. We all know the statistics about startups - that nine of ten fail in their first year. We have seen that even more predominantly in the press lately with the fallout of Dot.com Mania. It appears the press is more interested in reported failures now than successes. The tide has certainly turned from a year ago when anything the Internet touched turned to gold. Now those Internet dreams have tarnished and all that is left is a stigma that may deter people and turn good ideas away.

So how does an entrepreneur overcome the fear associated with those odds and trek on in the midst of widespread pessimism?

Well I think the best advice I can give to an entrepreneur is to fully test the business model before throwing millions of dollars at it. The problem with many of the failed Dot.com companies can be analyzed by looking at a company like Pets.com. The problem with Pets.com was that people fell in love with the sock puppet and forget to look at the hand behind it or the bottom line. It appeared to me that it was going to be difficult for this type of business to make money, especially with so many competitors. I wondered why their investors bought into their profitability analysis. I still don't know how they expected to be profitable when they sold their products below market rate and offered free shipping.

That company was funded on a promise that the world would come rushing to buy pet products online just because it existed. The belief that if you build it they will come has been the major fall of most failed Dot.coms. One other failed belief that Pets.com had is if you build it and spend bazillions of dollars on television commercials and billboards consumers will flock to your site. I went to the site once and bought some dog vitamins and that cute sock puppet. And that was all I visited - only once – and I loved that sock puppet! People are busy and it is incredibly hard to get them to change their patterns. Old habits die-hard and people did not rush to the Internet to buy things as companies and investors had planned.

I mention Pets.com but my own company had similar problems. I used Pets.com as an example because they are widely known (because of all those millions spent on television commercials). We faced challenges that were very similar. I brought in the Ivy League MBA's to do the business modeling analysis and they showed me that MsMoney would be a hugely profitable business. Well they told me what I wanted to hear and it just so happened that they believed it also. Unfortunately, it turned out to be overly optimistic analysis and therefore bad advice. The MsMoney.com business model was flawed from the very beginning and I should have opened my eyes and seen the real truth! But alas, I did not, so I spent millions of dollars believing in my dream, to only have it shattered nine months later when the revenues we predicted never showed up.

I was fortunate to be a creative and flexible individual so I was able to make some major changes to shift the business model in order to survive. But it wasn't easy. Luckily my tenacious personality wouldn't allow me to quit.

The advice I have for a new company is to start small because this will give you the opportunity to explore the market and turn consumer behavior theory into reality. Consumer behavior is hard to predict, so unless you have some solid measures of past performance it will be difficult to project future activity.

If you are not a consumer company and instead sell your products to businesses, then talk directly to the type of businesses you would be selling your product to. Get some verbal commitments that they would buy your product or service before you actually spend the money to build it. This might seem like common sense, but you would be amazed how much common sense was thrown out the window during the Dot.com heydays.

Above all, stay flexible. The New Economy is incredibly dynamic and requires leaders who can adapt quickly to changes. Most venture capitalists I have spoken to say that it is very common to start a company with a particular plan in mind only to shift the focus within the first year once more data starts filtering in. So be open to change and new opportunities and capitalize on what is working and don't dwell on what is not.

What personality traits and skills have you been known for over the course of your career?

The personality traits I have been known for are my optimism and tenacity. Regardless of the situations I have been faced with, I have been able to see the bright side and strategically plow ahead no matter what the circumstances were.

This is a quote I often think of when my hope falters.

"Most of the important things in the world have been accomplished by people who have kept on trying when there seemed to be no hope at all." - Dale Carnegie

Think of people like Benjamin Franklin, Christopher Columbus, Madam Curie and Helen Keller. The reason these people are remembered in history is because they have overcome obstacles and challenges and their courage has changed the world. What these people have in common is that they never gave up until they found the answer or solved their problem.

"No pessimist ever discovered the secrets of the stars, or sailed to an uncharted land, or opened a new heaven to the human spirit." - Helen Keller

Benjamin Franklin used to say when he was experimenting with electricity, "I haven't failed 1000 times, I have found 1000 ways that don't work, which has put me even closer to a solution."

Experience has taught me the difference between tenacity and stubbornness. I probably should not have been so stubborn believing that the first business model of MsMoney was viable. If I would have given up earlier on Plan A, I could have started on Plan B much sooner. It was Plan B after all that was the profitable plan. If I had converted to Plan B sooner, I would have avoided the frightening walk near bankruptcy. Of course, I was being tenacious when I forged ahead to create a Plan B and follow through with it even though success looked dubious from the start.

"Some people believe holding on and hanging in there are signs of great strength. However, there are times when it takes much more strength to know when to let go and then do it." - Ann Landers

I would have to say that my best skills are people skills. These are often difficult to describe because they are so complex. I take time to understand the psychology and motivation behind the people that I deal with, whether it is a team member of MsMoney or a business partner. If you don't understand the fundamentals of someone's personality than it is difficult to inspire or motivate that individual to seek their own success or success on your behalf. I try to treat each person as an individual and work to customize a management or business development approach to their unique style.

It is a lot easier to push a new plan through an organization if you get buy in from the managers who will be leading the teams. The more you can make the plan appear as if your plan is their idea, the higher your chances of success. Of course this isn't always easy and takes a lot of time. I have a small organization so I am able to spend quality time with my managers so that they can be empowered to make their own decisions that mirror company goals. With business partners it is always important to define what is in it for them. It is time to put them first and create strategies and plans that will help them succeed. That is how you get their attention. Once you have gotten them excited it is a lot easier to ensure that you will also win from their success.

How did you develop these skills?

I think my personality traits came from growing up in the Midwest and being instilled with a solid work ethic from a father who worked 80 hours a week and a mother who was the CFO of the household and lived life to its fullest. My tenacity comes from being surrounded by mostly boys as a child and always trying to keep up with their shenanigans even though I was much smaller.

My people skills come from being very social throughout every stage of my life. My more formal people skills came from observing sales representatives for years when I was working in marketing. I was often taken out to dinner by these folks and marveled how their lives seemed so affluent and stress free and how fun they were to be around. I decided I wanted to explore that lifestyle and eventually took a job in sales and went through some excellent formal sales training.

What training and life experience taught me is that, "Selling is not Telling." In fact, selling is 80% listening and 20% talking. It is amazing what you find out when you really listen to someone. People tell you what they need if you pay attention. But too often we don't listen and we miss this critical information. I also learned the ABC's (Always Be Closing), which is the motto of any good sales rep because they know that the quickest way to a sale is to have a plan of action that you stick to.

How do you become an executive/leader?

To be an executive you need to look at the bigger picture of the business. You have to look outside your job title and your role and see how the company is going to achieve its success or failure. You have to understand the dynamics of the industry and be able to adapt quickly to changes in the environment. You have to understand the psychology of the teams you are working with and what motivates them. You have to understand the psychology of your business partners and create a win-win situation for them so that both of you can succeed.

In many ways, you have to put your ego last, and understand that you are only as good as your team.

It is an incredibly tough role to be at the top. People are always looking to you for answers and sometimes you just don't have them. There are many executives who understand this and are afraid to ask for help and even worse there are those executives who think they have all the answers when they don't. A whole new crop of executive coaches has emerged to address these issues. I use one myself. They are invaluable helping me look outside of my circumstances and see clarity in simplicity when I could not find it myself.

The unfortunate thing about being a CEO is that everyone is looking to you for answers - not for questions. Your employees, your Board of Directors, your investors, and the press, are all looking to you for the vision and the blueprint for making the business a success. Who do you have to talk to? Not a lot of people. This is where executive coaches come in and can help you think through some of the tough questions you are facing and facilitate the process to an answer. They don't give you the answer, they just give you a flashlight to help you find it.

I am fortunate to have spent time with a professional executive coach. I also have an informal coach who happens to be my husband Hans Bukow. He is currently the CEO of his own company, eWork.com. He is also a fifteen year executive veteran of startups and has raised over twenty five million dollars for his ventures. I can go to him with my questions and he provides me not only a flashlight, but also a spotlight, since he knows me so well, and sometimes he even has the answers. This definitely makes my life easier.

True leaders are not born, they are made. Good leaders and executives learn from their mistakes and continue to grow as they acquire more experience. They look at obstacles as an opportunity to improve and then assimilate this information into their management "bag of tricks."

How important are setting goals? How often should you update them?

Most motivational speakers will tell you that setting goals and writing them down is the difference between success and failure. It is very hard to shoot for something if you don't even know what it is. I truly believe in setting goals and have done this since I was 12 years old. I have achieved most goals I set out to do including becoming a CEO.

The goals that I did not achieve turned out not to be right for me at the time. Even though I did not understand that then and was disappointed, I did not dwell on failure, I only focused on my next success. It is so important to move on - to look forward and not to look back and punish yourself for not being perfect. There were so many things I thought I wanted when I was younger, and now looking back, I realize that I am very lucky I did not achieve some of the goals I had early on in my career. I wonder what would have happened if I got the CD-ROM production job I wanted right out of Grad school. I might have been lulled into the secure corporate life and never headed out on my own to start my own company. Who knows? The idea though is to trust and have faith that things will happen as they are supposed to. If one door closes another one opens and it usually leads to a better place. Realizing this is the key to eliminating your fear of failure and optimizing the path to your dreams.

When I started setting goals so long ago, I had no life experience to show me that I could achieve any of them. Now my life experience has proved to me when I set a goal, I will achieve it, especially if it is "right" for me.

Haven't you heard before, "You need to be careful what you wish for because you just might get it." Keep this in mind before you set your goals. I had always said I wanted to be a CEO, but when I became one, I had to think twice if this is what I wanted to do for the rest of my career. It was so much more challenging and time-consuming than I expected.

You should update your goals when they are no longer fitting your needs. You have to make sure that you design a career and life that makes you happy. Because if you are not happy then you will not be at your peak performance and you are doing yourself and the company you work for a disservice. When you do something you love, everything snaps into place and work flows effortlessly. Don't forget this and change your goals when you start to realize you are struggling or aren't happy anymore and achieving your goal isn't likely to improve the situation.

I am in the process of refining my goals and trying to create more balance in my life. I started to realize that being a CEO for the rest of my career would not afford me the type of lifestyle where I could be truly happy. So my next step is to give up the reigns as CEO and act more as the visionary for my organization and Chairman of the Board.

What has been the best piece of business advice you have received along the way in your career?

Stick to what you do best. I know what my best skills are and yet I have put myself into too many situations that rely more on my weaknesses than my strengths. My life would be much easier if I could construct an environment that weighed more heavily on my stronger skills. I am in the process of designing the MsMoney team to augment it with people who are stronger at the skills I am weak at.

Granted you can always learn new skills and adapt your nature to adjust to your environment, but true peace comes when you use the skills that are more natural to your personality.

What has been the best piece of personal advice you have received along the way in your career?

Think twice before acting. Many people tend to want to act quickly to resolve a crisis situation and often don't think thoroughly through all the various paths. This is the time when a CEO has to be their best. They have to be calm under fire and behave the same way in the eye of the hurricane, where the skies are blue and the wind calm, as they do in the midst of the storm. I have the unique ability to maintain a clear head in some of the most dire work circumstances and project a sense of peace. This is so critical when in a challenging environment.

I still have room for improvement though. There are times where my emotions get the best of me (especially when it is not that important - like when I am on the phone with PacBell) and I may blurt something out without spending the time to realize how my comments might be interpreted. I have however improved tremendously in this arena over the last 10 years. Nothing like a little experience to prove that acting from your emotions can cause some real problems! (If you want PacBell to help you, then don't get angry and yell at them, that is the surest way to get your phones shut off!)

What additional advice do you have for women that will help them in their careers?

Be grateful for things that you already have. You might hope to have it all, but you don't have to have it all at one time. I look at my life and see how certain times I have felt I have had it all, and yet only years later my definition of having it all changed. So the best advice I can give is to be grateful for what you have at this time period of your life. The more you appreciate your current circumstance, the healthier you will be overall. You are more likely to attract additional good things to your life if you show gratitude for what you have accomplished so far.

I remember when I started my first business. Every time I acquired a new account I would internally feel gratitude and thankfulness for what I had achieved. I was still far from my final goals, but that doesn't mean I couldn't appreciate the goodness in my life at that moment.

Sometimes when I start to feel a little depressed, I open a bottle of nice Cabernet and pour two glasses, one for myself and one for my husband. I then light a candle and we sit on our living room coach to think about what we have in our lives to be thankful for. We take turns and say something we are thankful for this day and then "ching" our glasses to commemorate the toast. It is amazing if you think about it, how much you really have to be thankful for and how good you will feel after pointing it out. Don't be surprised if you finish your first glass of wine and you haven't run out of things to toast about!
Be dependable not only to yourself but also to others. Being dependable means that you follow through on your promises. If that promise is to yourself to take a few hours away to pamper yourself so that you can return to work more refreshed, then you must follow through. Being dependable to others is very important so that people can predict your behavior and rely on you to carry through. This is a lesson I learned at my very first job.

Be on time. I am never ever late (unless mother nature intervenes) because I feel this shows that I respect whoever is waiting for me and it begins to show my dependable nature. As a businesswoman, people will respect you if you respect their time.

What are the skills women should be learning right now in order to excel in the future?

Business Week once had a great article that says that women make better CEO's than men. The interesting thing is that the researchers were "startled" by the results since the studies weren't trying to prove that. Why do you think that is? I would have to say that I am a little startled by the results also. Now that I am a CEO I understand the challenges that a CEO faces. My initial impressions of being a CEO were that I had to be aggressive, controlling, competitive and THE problem solver. Not only is this behavior not in line with who I am truly am, but it was wrong and ineffective. This behavior, indicative of male CEO's, has been found by company evaluations to be the opposite of what is needed to succeed in the New Economy.

In fact, more creative, flexible and open leadership is needed to steer through the multiple obstacles that companies face when they are driving to success. Gone are the days of the typical male-centric military model where "the troops" are talked at and only provided information on a "need to know" basis. Today's worker, who is in high demand, expects open communication lines and demands to be listened to. The new breed of CEO's who can adjust to the new rules of bureaucracy are those which are most likely to succeed. It is now about learning to listen and creating harmony in the organization. It is about building teams and getting those members to buy in to the ideas generated at the top.

Team members who feel like management cares about them are less likely to jump to the next hot job offer that comes across their desk (and those offers will come). If employees are feeling valued and are happy they are much more likely to produce quality work. They want conflicts addressed immediately so that their peace is not disrupted. CEO's who can handle conflict are more likely to get better results from their people and lead a company to success. All of these skills mentioned above are much more likely to be the strengths of women and not men. Women are more likely to put personal glory aside and act on behalf of the larger organization. It is just this type of thinking that makes them better CEO's. The Business Week article quoted 4 different studies that showed that women were 50% - 85% better at the skills needed to survive in the New Economy than men. Some of those skills included: motivating others, fostering communications, producing high-quality work and listening to others.

Based on my experience, I would have to say once I spent more time mastering these skills instead of the original skills I thought I needed to have as a CEO, my organization was much more happier, healthier and successful.

We have another decade to determine if this is really true for the rest of the world. How many women do we think will be running the top 1000 corporations in the year 2010? If these studies were right, then I would expect more than six (which is how many are CEO's today).

What sort of opportunities does the "Internet Economy" present for women specifically?

The Internet economy has given me the opportunity to flourish. I was a pioneer in the fledgling New Economy and the world was my oyster. I had enormous opportunities open to me because the demand for those with my talent was extremely high. There was very little competition and the rules were not set yet so there was no predisposed gender bias. I still think there isn't.

What are some good resources for women?

I would recommend reading at least 1 book a month that is timely and relevant to your business because this is information you will be expected to know. You should also subscribe to at least 3 industry magazines and peruse them for relevant topics every week.

I also recommend reading topics that focus on the softer side of things at least once a week. Ideally this content should discuss motivation, inspiration and emotions. When you are an entrepreneur it is really easy to get yourself into a downward spiral and start thinking that you aren't really capable of being on your own and running a company. So you need to read something that has a lot of positive messages in it. If you listen to the news frequently, you will notice that you are constantly bombarded by negative messages that can have an adverse affect on your psyche and cause you to be more pessimistic than you normally would be. Scientists actually did studies to prove this. As a result, I usually won't watch programs with violence, and for that same reason, often won't even watch the evening news.

I enjoy books with inspirational quotes and motivational messages, especially content that gives the reader the sense that they are 100% in control of their environment. One of my favorite thoughts I have read is: Change your thinking, and you can change your life. You are in charge and you can achieve whatever you believe.

I have to be honest and say that my confidence and security comes from reading this type of material. I need these positive messages to keep me optimistic and upbeat. I definitely notice that when I take a few weeks or a month without centering myself with inspirational/motivational topics, that my enthusiasm starts to wane a bit and I start to get cynical. I call this stuff my happy drug! I need it to be at my best.

A friend of mine asked me after I launched the MsMoney.com website with the First Lady and a national TV crew, if I was afraid. I said no, of course not. But then I followed and said, "If I knew I had to rely on this one event to define my success, then that would be scary. Instead, I trust and have faith that no matter what I do, that things will always work out for the best. This is what makes me fearless and allows me to pursue all the dreams."

Ask yourself, "What would you do in your life if you knew you wouldn't fail?" Now go out there and do that! Don't be afraid!

How does someone overcome the fear of failure?

Better than a Mercedes
Or a jewel laded ring
Is the indelibly memory
Of a non-material thing

For lovely things come
With hearts full of hope
And you shouldn't worry
Or even stop to mope
There really is no such thing as failure
Nothing to get you down
It's all in your head
So put on your golden crown

If you interpret everything as alright
Then you will never experience the night
Up in the heavens you will soar
If you realize life isn't a chore

Come with me and experience the fun
Take your time there is no need to run
Stop and smell the roses and be full of smiles
The world is your oyster without all the guiles

Imagine that you are the highest kite that can fly
Your life will then be free from the heaviest sigh
If you want to live where fear has no rule
You can experience free living without being a fool

Because sooner or later
If you live without fear
You will always be full of good cheer
And you will accomplish everything that is dear
Nothing can be done with fear. Fear robs your energy and blocks you from achieving your goals. So take proactive steps to try to eliminate the fear in your life.

I created the poem as a simple piece to help people think about what is truly important in life. Is it the big house, the fancy car, the designer clothing? Is this how you strive to define yourself? I hope not, because if you do, there will always be more things to buy and more people who have more than you. Also, if you base your self-worth by the things you own, then they will end up owning

37

you instead. What happens if an earthquake eliminates all your possessions? (I think about that one since I live in the Marina in San Francisco.)

Think through what is important to you and by doing that you can start to more clearly define what you are really afraid of. Are you afraid your ego might get hurt? Do you define yourself strictly by your accomplishments and not by your values and integrity? Are you afraid of financial failure? Is it because you won't be able to own all those nice things and that is what you need to be happy?

Once you pinpoint what happens if you fail, you will be better prepared to determine if you can live with that result. If you are worried your ego might get hurt then don't take yourself so seriously!

I remembered the first time I learned to laugh at myself. I was about to move to San Francisco from Arizona and I wanted to get a nice new cosmopolitan hairstyle for my new job in the city. I thought I would get a trim and a perm to add some body to my hair, instead I got the perm from Hell. I went in with long straight blond hair and came out like a poodle that put their paw in an electric outlet. It was the worst thing you could ever imagine. Instead of leaving in tears and crying for the next few months, I laughed hysterically every time I looked in the mirror. It was so horrendous, how could I take my head seriously. I would make jokes about it to my friends and family, mostly so they wouldn't feel sorry for me. There was nothing to feel sorry about. I laughed when I met strangers because they probably thought I wanted my hair to look like that.

Well I survived and my hair grew out, and now when I think about the event I still smile. It is not the circumstances that create our happiness, it is our interpretation of them. I feel like a really learned a lesson then, I was 23 years old and I was just starting to learn to laugh at myself. It was a wonderful thing and became something I would apply to my career for the next 11 years as I struggled to reach my goals and cope with failure.

You have to stop being afraid of making mistakes. If I never made mistakes, I would never be where I am today. I feel like I have made them all! Ok, well most of them. Probably because I never really knew what I was doing, after all no one told me. I had to figure things out for myself. You have to remember: the greater the risk, the greater the reward. I would like to add to that: the greater the risk, the greater the mistakes, the greater the reward. If you aren't making enough mistakes, you probably aren't living your life to the fullest.

If you are afraid of financial failure, spend some time assessing the non-material things you value such as nature and friendships.

What I have done to overcome the fear of financial failure is to detach myself from material things. I learned my lesson early with this one. By the time I was 27, I was living in a million dollar home, had a brand new beautiful convertible, went on expensive vacations, drank the best wine and ate the best restaurants. By the time I was 28, I had absolutely none of that. The only thing I had left was a master's degree, a bunch of student loans and a lot of credit cards. I had seen all the material things disappear overnight with the "disappearance" (break-up) of my boyfriend. It was his stuff, not mine. That was how he defined himself, not me. Well granted, I did define myself by his stuff when I had it for the five years I was with him. I was young and naïve at one time. However, when I did not have it anymore, I had to redefine myself. I had to really decide what was important in my life and it wasn't what made up his life.

I rebuilt my life and my foundation with truly beautiful things that could not ever be taken away from me such as an appreciation of nature, a love of walking on the beach, good friends I could depend on, a family that loved me, a new career that I was passionate about and a value system that wasn't in conflict with my lifestyle. This is what changed my life. Once I detached myself from the material possessions I detached myself from the fear. After all, what did I have to lose now? I became grateful for each little thing that entered my life - a new computer, a new account, a new friend, a new plant, etc. I was living my life independently and loving every minute of it. From a materialistic standpoint, I only had a fraction of the "things" I was used to. But it didn't matter, I was happier.

I would rather live in a studio and have the freedom to explore the world with wonder, than live in a mansion full of servants and wonder at nothing.

The interesting thing is that once I let go and let life take its course, the material possessions starting appearing back in my life. The house, the car, the clothes, the vacations, etc. But this time, I was not attached to them. They could all disappear and I would be just fine. I even keep my old car around, even though I have a brand new shiny one worth ten times as much. I do this just to remind myself I would be happy driving anything and could live without all the possessions.

One of my favorite anonymous quotes is below.

"The soul would have no rainbow, if the eyes had no tears."

So go out there and live your life to the fullest and create some pain and sorrow - otherwise you won't even know what happiness is when you see it! Don't be afraid of the shadow of fear, it only means that there must be sunshine nearby casting it's light.

"I learned from experience that the greater part of our happiness or misery depends on our disposition and not on our circumstances." - Martha Washington

Where can an entrepreneur go for help?

I would have to attribute my success as an entrepreneur early in my career to the networking groups I belonged to. I was on the Board of Women In Communications and have participated in many different Internet networking organizations over the years. Most top-notch organizations have seminars they sponsor that can help you learn the skills you will need in that field. It is also a good chance to meet people in your industry.

The connections you make with people are very important if you are starting your own business. I can't emphasize this enough. My first dozen clients at Tiff.Com came from networking with women. Without networking and the support of women, Tiff.Com would have shut its doors and I would probably be working for some large corporation.

You can read a hundred books, but that isn't good enough, you need to put those theories into practice. Being part of a networking group helps you do this and test out new ideas and plans.

Mentoring can also play an important role in a woman's business career. I personally did not have any mentors - but I did surround myself with successful women who I met at networking events. Watching them gave me the confidence that I could be successful just like them.

I mentor a few fledgling entrepreneurs myself. It is a rewarding experience for both of us. Not only are they able to benefit from my knowledge and experience, but I also reap the rewards of learning through teaching. It gives me the opportunity to stretch my horizons and become involved in plans and ideas that I am interested in pursuing but don't have the time to execute myself. Mentoring keeps my strategic thinking muscles flexed and in good use. The old saying "use it or lose it" can certainly be applied to your brain.

I have also been exposed to educational seminars, networking and mentoring through a startup business incubator that MsMoney is part of. This special community is called the Women's Technology Cluster and it focuses on creating a positive environment for women entrepreneurs. Studies show that companies that are part of incubators have a higher rate of success than those that aren't. My experience shows me that this is most likely because of the community support that is provided by these organizations. Being able to share your experience and learn knowledge from those in a similar circumstance is very valuable. Also having the ability to network amongst a greater pool of professionals can mean the difference between closing that next twenty million dollars in financing or NOT. If you have the opportunity to be part of an organization like this I would recommend it.

What should women avoid in the business world?

I would purposely stay away from negative people whenever you can. It is so easy for someone to put your business plan or idea down. This is really hard to do when you are out pitching to venture capitalists (but that is another story). It takes the rare individual who can see the same pot and the end of the rainbow as you do. I find that I am often confronted with negative people and have to proactively deal with them. The worst scenario is when you find you have a negative person working on your team. That person's behavior can bring down a whole organization if not kept in check. What I usually do is try to confront the situation as soon as possible and turn around that individuals thinking. Or if that isn't working, I won't hesitate to ask them to leave my organization.

Another dilemma I have had is working on teams with clients where one of their team members has a negative disposition. This is more difficult to confront because you don't have any managerial control over their work or environment. This has not happened very often to me, but when it has, I have turned down future work from that client, because I will not subject myself, or my team to their negativity.

You only have one life to live, so you should fill it with as many positive experiences as possible. When you are confronted with negativity, don't just sit back and let it happen, do what you can to change the circumstances.

Keep in mind thought that not everything is in your control. Another one of my favorite quotes is below.

"Grant me the serenity to accept the things I can not change, the courage to change those I can, and the wisdom to know the difference."

What must women do differently than men in order to succeed?

Spend time learning the source of problems and not just trying to cover them up with a quick fix. Women are very good at this because they are more likely to initiate conversation to determine where the problems lie and are willing to talk about it. Corporations (mostly run by men) are very bad at this because it takes a lot of effort to fix big problems and it is easier to patch the symptoms than to treat the problem.

Women who want to "have it all" should draw this same analogy into their personal lives. Because you can't be your best in the work place if your home place is out of order. Women are much more prone to talk about their issues and to seek self-help advice than men. So we should use this tendency to our advantage. Men, in their personal lives, are more likely to run from conversation and introspection and buy flowers hoping that roses will fix everything.

The issues we face as women can be daunting. We are under so much pressure to be perfect at everything we do - the perfect executive, the perfect wife, the perfect mother, the perfect daughter, etc. Sometimes it is hard to keep up with these predefined perceptions the world places on us and we often become disillusioned.

"Show me a woman who doesn't feel guilty and I'll show you a man." - Erica Jong, Writer

Aren't we always feeling guilty about something? If you spend too much time at work, you feel guilty you are not spending enough time at home. When you spend too much time at home, you feel like you are not spending enough time at work. When you do too much for others you feel like you should spend more time on yourself. When you spend any time on yourself you feel selfish. Yikes! How do we survive and feel like we can have it all?

It is not easy because our own bad habits and negative thinking often hold us back. We usually try to treat the symptoms that arise, instead of treating the underlying problem that is causing these surface symptoms to appear over and over again. Guilt might be the real problem in our life and a symptom might be something like depression, weight gain, or insomnia, which we then might try to treat with a quick fix such as compulsive shopping (retail therapy) and diet or sleeping pills. What we get as a result might temporarily fix the depression and weight gain, but we also end up with more problems such as debt and poor health. Not at all what we intended.

We spend our lives trying to patch up these small symptoms and the minute one goes away another one crops up. It is an endless cycle - so what is the point? Stop dealing with the symptoms and take the time to figure out what is really the underlying problem manifesting this behavior. This is NOT an easy process and it takes a lot of courage to look at your flaws straight in the face. It is a lifelong journey into your psyche and soul, but the benefits of freeing yourself from the things weighing you down will allow you to soar through life with unbounded happiness and enter your own Utopia.

I know what my underlying problems are and how they manifest themselves in my life. They say that identifying and admitting the problem is the first step to helping cure it. I also understand that I am not perfect and that healing myself is a long journey that will take my time and attention. In the meantime while I walk down that path to self-actualization, I still have to cope with some of the annoying little symptoms and forgive myself for not having all the answers.

Meg Ryan sums up a great way of thinking, "Oh, I'm so inadequate - and I love myself!"

"Face your deficiencies and acknowledge them, but do not let them master you. Let them teach you patience, sweetness, insight. When we do the best we can, we never know what miracle is brought in our life, or in the life of another." - Helen Keller

What are some good ways to relieve stress?

Eat Right. This is so important. You need your energy if you are "doing too much." Okay, even I don't have the time to eat right sometimes, but I always take my vitamins. So find yourself a good antioxidant multi-vitamin and take it every day.

Drink lots of water. You have heard this over and over - 8 glasses a day. I probably drink 10 glasses a day. Yes you will have to go to the bathroom all the time, but it is well worth it. You need to stay hydrated to have energy and to flush out all those antioxidants caused by stress.

Breath. How often when you are stressed do you actually hold your breath? This is the worst thing you can do. Take a deep breath and let it out. All of a sudden things seem better. My husband is always making fun of me when I let out these huge sighs. I don't even notice I am doing it half of the time. It is a natural mechanism for me now so that when I am stressed, I sigh deeply.

Stretch. Most people carry their stress in the neck and back which can really make you cranky at the end of a long day. So wake up and stretch those neck and back muscles for 10 minutes. Stretch another 5 minutes in the middle of the day and 10 minutes when you get home. If I forget to stretch because I am rushing into my day, my dog always reminds me. The first thing she does when she gets up from sleeping the night, or even a nap, is stretch. First she puts her paws way out in front of her and her head low to the ground. Then she stretches the left foot way out, then the right foot, and then puts her butt way up in the air. Same thing every time, she never forgets. How does she know to stretch and most people don't?

Work out. This is the best thing for me when I start getting anxiety from having too much to do. I have all this nervous energy and I need to get it out somehow. Nothing like thirty minutes on the Stairmaster to get the endorphins flowing and my brain cells sharpened.

Smile. Also, relax your face, open your jaw and move it around. Start to feel the muscles loosen and then settle on a neutral uplifting position. Scientists have proven that the physical act of smiling creates positive feelings in your brain. How is that for a quick fix?

Soak in the tub. My favorite thing to do at the end of the day. I just imagine all those cares and worries melting away in the heat and washing down the drain. Calgon take me away!

Light a candle. Or if you can, build a fire in your fireplace. Just watching the flames trickle and flick randomly around the logs (or the candle) will help connect you with nature and disconnect you from work.

Listen to Music. Really listen to it and pay attention to the rhythm, the instruments, the words. Depending on your mood - sometimes you want it loud and upbeat, sometimes you want it soft and soothing. Music helps me escape my immediate reality and places me in another world without a To Do list. I recommend listening to classical music - this will help you exercise your mind.

Be nice. Do something nice for someone and notice how good you will feel.

Think about the Universe. There are 150 billion stars in the sky and a billion other galaxies in our Universe. There are stars exploding into supernovas and collapsing in black holes. There is beauty and mystery in the infinite. Now think about the problem facing you. Doesn't seem so humongous anymore does it? I have always loved Astronomy and Carl Sagan because they help me put my life in perspective within the Grand Life of the Universe.

Walk on the beach. I do this one a lot. The soothing sound of the water lapping on the sand will wash away your troubles. Think about how the tides may change but things fundamentally stay the same and the sun will always come up tomorrow.

Walk in the woods. Enjoy the majestic trees and the delicate plants and appreciate the harmony of life. These plants are breathing in our carbon dioxide and turning it into oxygen so we can then breath it again; a nice a simple symbiotic relationship.

Go to a Library. Being surrounded by peace and quiet can be wonderful all by itself, but you are also surrounded by thousands of years in knowledge.

Wear comfortable clothes. What is the first thing you do when you get home after work? Put on comfortable clothes right? What about wearing comfortable clothes to work.

Look at pictures of happy memories. I tend to do this more often when my husband is away on business for a long time. I have a photo album of my favorite pictures of him during our fun-filled adventures. They always make me smile.

Slow down. This is by far the toughest one for me. My brain is whirling at a hundred miles a minute, I am not happy if I am not multitasking. I talk fast, I type as fast as I talk, I walk fast, read fast, eat fast - and I should slow down? Yes. Not only should I slow down, but I also can't expect the world to operate as quickly as I do. Patience is a virtue and it is something I have to work hard at.

Do women have to make sacrifices to have a successful career?

Being a married woman in my 30's, I am faced with the difficult decisions of creating life balance and starting a family. I will definitely have to make sacrifices in my career so that I can accomplish these personal goals. Right now I spend 90% of my energy on my career and I really don't have room for much else. I will eventually have to drop that to 50% so that I can live a more balanced life. It doesn't mean that my career will stop being successful, it just means that the ways I define success in my career will have to change.

Is there any way to have children and still be on an "executive track?" How do you go about doing this?

This is the biggest challenge I will be facing in the next few years. I brought a dog into my life so that I could begin to understand some of the issues involved in the care and feeding of something besides myself. I take her to work every day but have so little time to interact with her. When I don't spend at least an hour of quality time with her a day (which believe it or not is sometimes difficult to spare), she gets very ornery and misbehaves. This is a great lesson for me as I approach Motherhood. I can't possibly work as much as I do and raise a healthy and happy child. So I will have to learn to redefine my role as an Executive. It doesn't mean I stop being an Executive, it means I have to set boundaries and times for being an Executive and times and boundaries for being a Mother. Being a parent truly is like having a second job and it needs equal time and attention. Right now my time and attention is only on MsMoney.

What rules do you think women should follow to be successful?

"If you obey all the rules, you miss all the fun." - Katherine Hepburn

"The thing that women have got to learn is that nobody gives you power. You just take it!" - Roseanne Barr

My advice - create your own rules. And read the book "Bad Girls Guide to Getting What You Want" for a little humor.

What advice do you have for women just starting their careers?

Live by example, it will have much more impact that any words you could impart.

Remember that happiness is not a destination but a way of traveling.

Do something you love!

You will notice as you progress in your career and have added life experiences that you will become more discontented with the status quo. As you mature you are more likely to start challenging commonly held perceptions and will aspire for a better way. This is probably why many women start their own businesses later in their career. Women are leaving the corporate world at twice the rate of men because they are getting fed up with the system.

What advice do you have for women who are out striving to succeed and have it all?

Executives get so caught up in the details of living that they forget to live. I had this problem as the CEO of MsMoney. I spent all my time and energy trying to ensure MsMoney's success and sacrificed everything else in my life. How could I have realistically expected that this would make me happy? I regret now not relying more on my friends to pull me up during my times of weariness. When you make it to the top of the Executive ranks, you start to adapt this, "I can do everything myself attitude." This can lead to loneliness if you don't balance it with healthy and nurturing relationships. You don't have to go it alone. Typically those who have made it to the top have had some sort of support system. Find out what yours is and use it when you need it.

Friends are there when you are weary and their influence can flavor your life with sunshine. Just two years prior to starting MsMoney, when my former business, Tiff.Com, was at its peak, I put it all aside to take a year off around the world for my honeymoon. Many people commented that they would never consider taking this time off at the most critical period of their career and especially when the Internet was so HOT.

I remember how hard I worked to get Tiff.Com where it was. It took years and a lot of risk and learning to get to that point. Was I to give it all up? I thought, what if I can't duplicate the same success when I returned? What if people don't take me seriously because I did this? I agonized at times over the decision. But when it came down to it, my new fiancé and I agreed that starting our lives together with a year trip around the world would be an unforgettable experience and would build a foundation and bonds between us that would last a lifetime.

"When two people love each other, they don't look at each other, they look in the same direction." - Ginger Rogers

Hans and I were looking in the same direction and we both put our successful careers on hold and risked everything for this trip. Fundamentally we kept our faith that when we returned, we would continue being entrepreneurs and spend our time working for causes that we were passionate about. We ignored the warnings of friends and family and headed out on our personal adventure. We stood for what we believed in, regardless of what others said, because opinions are generally a fleeting thing, but our values are forever.

The world trip was the most amazing experience of my life and we have two thousand pictures and forty hours of video to look back upon. We even created a website that contained our photos and stories. I am currently writing a book about it called "The Millennium Odyssey – Discovering the 7 Wonders of the New World."

We returned safely home a year later and luckily the Dot.com mania had even picked up speed. We had no problem raising excitement and money for our new ventures.

So, why when I became a CEO of my new venture, hadn't I learned from the world trip experience and strove to create some sort of balance in my life? It appeared that I was an "all or nothing" kind of person. It was difficult to find the middle road between taking a year off and working intensely seventy hours a week. I finally starting to realize, at 34 years old, that having it all meant that different pieces of it will appear at different periods of my life, and when I started to approach the end of my days, what I will be left with would be a beautiful and self-fulfilling picture.

"At the end of your life you will never regret not having passed one more test, not winning one more verdict, or not closing one more deal. You will regret time not spent with a husband, a friend, a child, or a parent." - Barbara Bush

"We must know that we have been created for greater things, not just to be a number in the world, not just to go for diplomas and degrees, this work and that work. We have been created in order to love and to be loved." - Mother Teresa

What inspires you to strive towards such difficult career goals?

I am inspired by people who have overcome enormous obstacles on their way to achieving success. I have a lot of respect for Senator Hillary Rodham Clinton because of her strength and courage. Consider everything that she survived as the First Lady and her grace in handling various situations with the press and the public. Most people would shrink from society, but instead she dusted off the debris and moved on and did not let it stop her. The fact that she had the tenacity and optimism to pursue her own dreams without letting the masses get her down is amazing. The fact that she won the New York Senate race even though people constantly told her she wouldn't is a testament to the fact that we as women are incredibly resilient and can accomplish anything we put our minds to.

"A woman is like a teabag, you don't know her strength until she is in hot water!" - Nancy Reagan

I often have people come to me to ask me how I overcame such odds to get where I am today. They want to know how they could possibly achieve a fraction of what I have and what has inspired me to keep pushing along even though I had so many obstacles. I like to bring up that there is nothing unique about me except my undying commitment to achieve what I set out to do. And the fact that I truly believe I can accomplish it regardless of the odds. I try to convince people that they can do anything they set their mind to. Why not?

Think about Helen Keller and the odds she overcame in her life. She was deaf and blind and diagnosed as being without intelligence. She didn't let others "opinions" of her stop her from living life to the fullest with whatever gifts she did posses. This is someone that didn't live in bitterness that she was robbed of her sight and her hearing, instead she moved passed that and used her other senses and faculties to explore the world in wonder. I quote her numerously throughout my writing because she has such an inspirational story to tell. No obstacle I have ever overcome has been of the same magnitude as hers.

Don't be afraid to follow your dreams even though the obstacles seem too much. I would never be where I am today if I believed only what OTHERS told me I would achieve. It is your life and you are the only one who can decide how you want to live it. So get started.

Tiffany Bass Bukow is the CEO and Founder of MsMoney.com, Inc., a company operating along two distinct lines of business. First is www.msmoney.com, a site whose mission is to empower women to become financially healthy that is part of a network of 2 million visitors. In addition, MsMoney has a consulting division dedicated to providing financial content and front-end design solutions to the banking industry. Tiffany develops and directs MsMoney's strategic business, marketing and technology initiatives. Tiffany is a leading expert in web development, instructional design, and marketing online

Prior to MsMoney.com, Tiffany founded an Internet Consulting company called Tiff.Com and served as President for 5 years. At Tiff.Com, she led a team of 20 professionals in the design, development and programming of web sites for industry leaders such as America Online, Sun Microsystems, Lucent and Bechtel.

Tiffany is an acclaimed international speaker and has been featured at Internet industry conferences, marketing forums and women's events. She has been quoted in the Wall Street Journal, Fortune, Business 2.0, Barrons, Working Woman and MSNBC and has appeared on television networks such as ABC and PBS. She has also hosted a weekly financial radio show called MoneySense for Sony's Redband Radio.

She holds an M.A. in Instructional Technologies and Multimedia from San Francisco State University and a B.S. in Business from the University of Arizona.

PATRICIA DUNN
Becoming a Leader
Barclays Global Investors
Global Chief Executive Officer

Tell me about your background and how you ended up where you are today.

I was a liberal arts major in college in the early 1970s with visions of following in the steps of Woodward & Bernstein as a political journalist who helped to change the world. I was basically a child of the '60s, having moved to the SF area at the start of high school, growing up in the era of "flower power" and the war protests. In college I had no conception of a business career and probably would have disbelieved entirely the outcome of my post-university years.

I graduated from the University of California at Berkeley in December, 1995, took a break for Christmas and started work at Wells Fargo Bank as a temporary secretary on January 2, 1976. My mother was a widow who had no training in the work world and was in financial distress, and my little brother was in grammar school. I needed a job quickly to support myself and help them, but figured on working for a year or two as a "temp" while I built up my credentials as a journalist. It was a nice idea, but completely impractical - but I only admitted this two years later, when Wells Fargo insisted I become a permanent employee because my tenure as a temp was breaking all the rules.

By that time, however, I was bitten by the bug of a different kind of revolution than the one I had intended to be part of as a muckraking journalist - the investment management revolution. I discovered I was working with some of the most brilliant and committed "revolutionaries" of the day, whose zeal and vision was infectious. Once I figured out I could, in my self-taught way, learn enough about what they were doing to help them, I was eager to be part of their team.

Over the years I've had the opportunity to work in many different aspects of investment management at the company that is now called Barclays Global Investors, learning more every day. I ended up running the company, to my surprise, but the privilege of doing so is something I think about every day.

Tell me a little bit about what you enjoy most about what you're doing right now.

It's the opportunity to shape the future of a worthwhile business, one that does great things for its clients, and rewards its people. The opportunity to have an impact is a lot of fun. The chance to work with people who are outstanding and are passionate about the business is very satisfying as well.

How do you create the right balance between not getting overloaded being in an executive position with so much going on? How do you manage everything you have to do on a daily basis?

I'm not sure I do. I am a big believer in delegation and I try to surround myself with people who do certain things a lot better than I do. I let them get on with it and that essentially creates my focus, which is to try and do the things that only I can do. I am an independent and relatively self-sufficient person, so this is something I have to continue to work on. Usually my first instinct is to do a lot of things myself, but there's only so much that one person can do. I try to focus on the things that nobody else will or should do if I don't do them. That's what I try to keep in mind.

When you do delegate to people what is it that makes you comfortable delegating to certain people? What are their skills or strengths that give you confidence in terms of delegating to them?

Initially you have to take a bet on people because, until they have built a track record of delivery and results, you're going on instinct more than anything else. It is very possible for people to be successful in one organization and then when they go to a new organization their track record doesn't follow them because of the environment and other influences. The business itself may not be as conducive to their best performance, but having said that, what gives me confidence to delegate is my experience with people and their delivery. It's easier and easier as you get stronger and stronger people around you.

What have you been known for over the course of your career?

I seem to be known mostly for having been a good salesperson and for being a good people manager. I thought I was a good quantitative portfolio manager, but no one seems to remember that so maybe I wasn't! I think the skills underpinning sales, client service and people management are to some extent transferable - both are about understanding and finding ways to meet the needs of others, whether they're customers or employees. I feel comfortable delegating a lot of authority to the right people, and have focused heavily on attracting the best talent to the business. As we have built the company outside the US, I have very consciously sought to develop my understanding and skills in the "multi-cultural" dimension, which I find very stimulating and challenging. In the last few years I have also tried purposefully to build my skills in financial management, technology and strategy. I find the best way to do this is to hire the best people in these areas and then learn from them.

How did you develop these skills?

I think some skills are innate, or hard-wired. I could never be an effective quantitative researcher, for example, because I just don't have the capability. On the other hand, communicating comes easily to me, which is the core skill of sales and people management. As to other skills, almost everything I have learned has been through observing others who have the various skills to manage a company, and I've had the luck to be around a lot of them.

What has been the best piece(s) of business advice you have received along the way in your career?

I don't think I've received much advice per se, but I have received a lot of encouragement, both from people I have worked for, and people who have worked for me. I've never felt I had to be someone I am not, and the best advice I could have received would be to work with one's strengths and shore up the weaknesses by putting the right team in place. I think people are very tuned-in to authenticity in others, particularly others in positions of "power," and they don't trust people whose behavior seems unnatural, forced or put-on. Fortunately I've worked over the years with open-minded people who have accepted my limitations - such as lack of formal training in finance - and encouraged me to accomplish whatever I can.

What has been the best piece(s) of personal advice you have received along the way in your career?

My husband has been a great advisor, and his refrain is "do all you can but don't worry if you can't do more." This is very balancing and helpful advice to anyone who is continually stretched to find the time to do everything one wishes, and do it all with excellence. I don't always find it easy to accept this advice, but I know it is right.

How important are setting goals? How often should you update them?
I feel leery about giving advice on this one - I have never been much of a goal-setter myself. I have always just wanted to be around and to demonstrate excellence on behalf of a business that delivers strong value to its customers, people and shareholders. Certainly every year I set goals on behalf of the company, but I never have had career goals per se.

What advice would you have for women trying to succeed in the business world?

My advice to women (and men) in business is this:

• Always work for someone whose success you can support enthusiastically, and do your best to help them succeed. Don't focus in the short run on your own career and markers of whether you're getting ahead - if you burden your boss with ongoing concerns of whether you are succeeding in your career, it drags both of you down.
• The converse, of course, is to move on as expeditiously as possible if you find yourself working for someone about whose success you are apathetic.
• Avoid "emotional blackmail" in your dealings with management. (Women do tend to have greater access to their emotions!) Try to control your emotions in tough situations. If you find yourself unable to do so, and end up displaying raw emotion in some way, don't beat yourself up - just go back when you are calmer and ask to have the conversation over again.
• Work for an organization whose products and/or services you can be proud to support. This allows your energy and skill to be truly unleashed, a requirement for success in any endeavor.

Do women have to make sacrifices to have a successful career?

We all have to make choices in life - men, too. In my view, the dual-high-powered career marriage with children is tough to pull off with grace and equanimity. It makes a big difference when there is economic wherewithal to hire people to help the family function well. The couple needs to be very clear on their priorities and not overwhelm their lives with commitments apart from business and family. I had four stepchildren, who lived mostly with my husband

and me, and a dual-career marriage. While the children were growing up, we took on virtually no commitments outside home and business. We survived mostly because my husband is incredibly supportive and calm. A highly-placed executive I know has five children, a husband in a demanding executive position, community involvement -and she makes it all look easy by prioritizing very well and being a great time manager and having lots of help. But if you don't have the support system, including the complete support of your partner, I don't think the career/family choice makes for a very pleasant life.

Is there any way to have children and still be on an "executive track?" How do you go about doing this?

I think the secret is to make business and family the absolute priorities and make sure the partners in the relationship are absolutely clear they are prepared to deal as real partners to make it happen.

Did you have mentors and people that helped guide you along your career path?

This is a question I get asked all the time. I think it's relatively uncommon that careers are coached along by an individual or two. I think you have to be mentored on a 360 basis from peers and subordinates. If you're lucky you will work for people in your career that you can learn from, as well as superiors. Their success becomes a motivator to you. Even if they don't take the stance as a mentor and make it clear that your success is part of theirs, you can still benefit from watching people you admire and learn from them. To me that's what mentoring is. It's learning by observing.

What were the most important things that you learned from these people?

I've learned everything I know from other people so it's hard to narrow the list. I wasn't born knowing what I know now, so I had to learn it from other people. There's a certain amount that I learned from reading, and some people learn better from that mode and some people learn better from experience. I think most people learn best from experience. I think you need to be lucky to have a successful business career because the experiences that you have and the people that you have them with are to a pretty large extent unmanageable. I've learned everything from how to conduct a board meeting to how to approach business strategy to how to give a motivational speech, by watching others do it.

Tell me what you've learned from reading. What types of things do you like to read in order to expand your knowledge base?

I like to keep very current with what's going on in our industry. I'll at least glance at any periodical or newspaper that is geared to the financial services and investment management industry. I think another aspect of success is that if you seriously enjoy what you do, you will find yourself reading those things while on vacation, not because you have to, but because you want to. If you're curious and interested about your business, you can accumulate a lot of information and knowledge about it just because you're driven to that kind of material.

People in general aren't always able to be doing what they want to be doing. When and if you were in those positions, how did you see the other side of it and keep yourself focused so you could take that next step later on?

I actually never was in a position that I dreaded being in. I have had days that I wish would pass quickly, but there was never really a time when I found myself kind of itching to move into a different role.

What advice would you give to other people who are in a position that they don't like?

My advice would depend upon whether it's the position in an organization that's the problem or whether it's the organization.

Let's say it's an organization you like, but it's a position that you're just not enjoying or there are just certain aspects that you really don't like.

That's the trickier one because you obviously want to preserve your reputation for being committed, loyal, not high maintenance and that sort of thing. I've certainly been around situations with people working, in some cases for me, who were looking to move into another position for whatever reason. I think it can be handled in a way that enhances an individual's reputation and actually helps advance their career by virtue of the fact that they handle this difficult situation very professionally. The key to it is to not hold a gun to anyone's head. You need to be clear about what it is that you want to move on to, and need to work with your management directly and try and make that happen. If it doesn't and can't be done because your direct manager, for example, is the problem, it can still be handled in a way that leaves everybody feeling okay. All you have to do is ask your manager if you can have a conversation with his or her manager together. At that point the senior manager is likely to get a positive impression from someone who's trying to handle the situation with the best interest of the company and yet is taking charge of their career. Those are ways to demonstrate high potential. I think it's an opportunity as much as anything else. If you have two layers of bad management, it's probably a sign that there's something wrong with the company and that gets a little trickier.

How important has networking been for you? In your opinion what's the right way to go about it?

I have to admit that I've never been much of a networker or a joiner. In part I think it's because the company that I'm with has always been something of a challenger of convention in this industry. We've grown as a result of taking positions that are seen as hostile to the rest of our industry. Networking from the position of outsider is more difficult, but by the time you have 20 years in an industry, you inevitably build up a whole raft of business contacts, clients, former clients, employees and former employees. You really have to fence yourself off not to have a network after a while.

When you're hiring people and you're looking to build a team around you, what impresses you on somebody's resume?

Until I meet a person I tend not to be particularly impressed one way or the other by a resume. I found a very high correlation between people who have been very accomplished academically and those who have achieved excellence beyond their academic career. On the other hand, I don't rely on academic credentials. I've hired people at the most senior levels who have very unimpressive educational backgrounds, but are clearly great achievers. If there's one thing on a resume that catches my eye, it's usually someone who has distinguished themselves academically.

What kind of advice would you give younger women?

One of them is paradoxical to becoming a leader, but has much wisdom in it, and that is "to lead is to serve." Most people at every stage who are ambitious, whether they're just out of university or further in their career, tend to underestimate how far they can get by serving their leaders and showing leadership by doing that. I think any chief executive is put off by people who are solely focused on their top priority being the level of attainment they have in their career. You do have to get out of yourself to be a leader and if you're obsessed with your own success, it poses quite a barrier to succeed. The analogy I'll use is a man or a woman who is desperate to get married. The odds are they are their own worst enemy in accomplishing that goal. If you find someone who's desperate to succeed, the same principle applies. I would advise, "Be a learner." The best thing you can do to be successful is to find something to do, an organization, a product, a service, anything that you are passionately interested in. Learn as much as you can about how to make that product or service successful in its marketplace. Believe me, people who have positive impact on achieving a company's goal are noticed.

Over the course of a career regardless of the stage you're at, how important is it to keep learning and what are the ways to do that? Is it putting yourself in new situations or different roles within the company?

You've just named two of them. Willingness to move laterally is a signal of the ability to lead. It means to management eyes someone who is a able to cope comfortably with uncertainty, is willing to put themselves in a new situation even if they're not the expert, has confidence and is committed to the success of the organization. If these things are true, a lateral move is the best opportunity to learn. Then I would also advise that there is as much to learn about any company from outside the walls of that company as inside. I'm always very impressed, for example, when very busy people nonetheless manage to make a contribution to the industry in general.

What do you feel has been your biggest strength or what's helped you the most along the way in terms of becoming a leader?

A leader must initiate, unite and inspire. I practice these skills every day. Another "core competence" of leadership is optimism, which is the opposite of cynicism. Optimism and confidence are, I believe, highly correlated and I am reflexively optimistic. I can get along well with all different kinds of people except cynics!

How do you become a C-level employee/leader?

I think you have to have a combination of talent, commitment, energy, and luck to become a leader. I know from my own experience that you can never tell who has the potential to be an executive or leader, because I certainly would never have been picked out for the role during the first few years of my career.

You just never know who can step up to the plate. It's always better to have the training and credentials, and those who have leadership as a goal in business should definitely seek them. Having some core skills that allow you to make an impact early in your career is very helpful, whether it's sales, technology, technical skills - but best always if they are accompanied by good "people" skills. Then, working for people and an organization you really believe in is key to career success. Finally, keep your fingers crossed because a lot of what happens along the way is completely uncontrollable.

What are the three most important things it takes to succeed on both a business and personal level in the 21st century?

- Ability to initiate ideas and strategies, unite people behind accomplishing them and inspiring them to make their best contributions
- Complete integrity
- Flexibility and resilience in the face of uncertainty and change

Patricia Dunn first joined the Barclays Group on its acquisition of Wells Fargo Nikko Investment Advisors at the end of 1995. In her role as chairman, she directs the development of BGI's global business strategy and oversees the management of BGI's businesses in the Americas, Europe, Japan, the Capital Markets Group, and activities in the areas of risk management, advanced active and index investments, and strategic planning. Since joining the business in 1976, she has served in a variety of roles at BGI and its predecessor companies, including consulting, portfolio management, trading, marketing and client relationships. She is a non-executive director of Hewlett-Packard Company.

VIVIAN BANTA
Career Transitions
Prudential Individual Financial Services
Chief Executive Officer

What have been some of your biggest hurdles and greatest joys you've had in your career?

I got into executive management really quite by accident. I started my career as a Programmer Analyst, building business applications for a worldwide bank. I was promoted very quickly into management, and seem to have taken to management like a duck takes to water. I was very lucky and kept taking on larger and larger responsibilities. I was catapulted into executive management while working for Bank of America in San Francisco. They felt it was important to build general management competencies for those individuals who they thought had high potential as leaders. Fortunately, I happened to be one of those individuals, and this was really a rather select group. As a result, I was plucked out of these technical disciplines and given a different set of opportunities. . For the first couple of assignments, I was truly terrified because I didn't have any background in the areas. I learned pretty quickly that common sense is common sense and you can apply it just about every place. The major difference is the opportunity to leave technical assignments and take on general management responsibilities, including   rotations around the company that gives you the bigger picture. As time went on, the responsibilities grew and so did the challenges. That's really how it all started.

Do you think having that technical background was an advantage?

Yes. It can be an advantage and it can be a disadvantage.   Having a technical background has served me well, but sometimes it doesn't serve others well at all.   Let me explain. It was an advantage for me because it taught me a very valuable skill, namely, how to think logically and how to gradually decompose problems and arrive at a solution. Problem solving is almost second nature to me, and that's an invaluable skill to have when you're in business.   Recently I was going through feedback that I had asked my direct reports to fill out on me. It was interesting to hear their comments in a variety of areas, but one of the things that came out very strongly was conceptual thinking, being able to take things that are unclear to many people and peel them apart until you can create clarity. I know I've developed those skills from my days on technical assignments.

That same technical background, by the way, can serve some people very poorly, because they will use that technical background to hide behind. What do I mean? I mean they will use their profession as an excuse for not learning how to communicate with people. They'll speak in jargon as a way to not have to explain things clearly and as a way to separate themselves from others. In my case, I was very lucky, and I extracted from my technical assignments what I thought were some excellent skills, which are still paying off for me. But it was painful. I didn't just slide into executive management easily.

How easy or hard is it to transition into something else, and how did you do it so successfully?

It's really about what your skills are and knowing your own strengths and weaknesses. Fortunately, the skills that I had were the same skills required to do different jobs. For example, people management skills are important in any transition. So is the ability to work with different kinds of people, the ability to build teams, the ability to question people, and the ability to solve problems. Those are skills that are transportable to any job, whether it's a job that you have a lot of background in or it's something you know very little about. I would rely on those basic skills and just take them with me everywhere I went. Clearly, as time went on, I fine tuned them and developed them more fully, but that's really how I did it. Analytical skills, conceptual thinking skills, and problem solving skills are the skills you need no matter what you do.

Goals are also very important, especially since the business world is one that is constantly in a state of change. Goals are a great way to personally challenge oneself to reach a new level. And goals need to be reevaluated and changed pretty frequently to keep up with the changes occurring in the marketplace.

You talk about learning and how important it is to keep learning. As you advance in your career how do you force yourself to keep learning?

I don't have to force myself to keep learning. Every day I get up out of bed, I learn something new. It's my lifeblood. I like to be challenged. I like to take something away every day that I've learned, whether it's about a person, process, business, concept, or philosophy. That's what keeps me energized. I'm very inquisitive, and I very much like to get to the bottom of things quickly. I like to understand things that I think are important, so with a personality like that I find myself in a position where I'm always learning, no matter what I do.

Everyone in business should be learning all the time. It doesn't matter if you're a CEO or a front-line worker. Knowledge fuels the brain. As a general rule, many women could benefit from additional training related to communication. I'm not talking about learning how to speak fluently, but I am referring to the power of persuasion and the art of negotiation. These are critical skills for today's marketplace, but they can also be applied to your own life.

How important is it for women to force themselves into new positions and learn new things?

It's very important because the business world changes every second, and you must keep your mind open and refreshed in whatever fashion you choose to do it in. Whether it's going to structured classes, reading books, or talking to people, you have to do these things, because if you don't, it doesn't take very long before you're just out of it. Things are changing so quickly, whether it's lifestyles, business trends, the stock market, or products, you really have to have a willingness to take in all of this information and do something with it that's proactive and positive. I always say to people, "If you don't like learning, if you don't have an open mind, or if you're not willing to deal with ambiguity, then you probably would not make a very good leader."

In addition, I would pass on a really great piece of advice I received early on in my career and I've used continuously: never let an organization's structure get in the way of achieving results. I've found that one needs to operate inside and outside of the structure, with a positive attitude, always moving forward, filling in the gaps wherever needed.

What about others impresses you, whether they're other leaders, people that work for you, people that you work for, or just people you know in general?

I have had the good fortune to work with some people who I thought were excellent leaders. They have vision, they have courage, and they don't let things that normal human beings do deter them off their path. They rise above little things that most people would get upset by. They know who they are. They're very open about their strengths and weaknesses, they don't try or pretend to be the most intelligent person, they are in touch with themselves, they are willing to take calculated risks, they have really excellent people skills, and they're able to talk to all kinds of people whether they're clerical people or senior executives. That's a real skill.

In addition, great leaders achieve great results and demonstrate good business sense. That summarizes for me what is impressive about other great leaders.

Anyone on the path to becoming a leader encounters numerous challenges. Tell me about some of the challenges that you've had or that people often face and what it takes to overcome them and learn from them?

There are so many challenges. For me the biggest challenge always is getting the right people. It's not that it's hard acquiring them, but making sure that they are the right person in terms of their skill set for the job, the right person in terms of what needs to be done, and the right person in terms of their willingness to work with the rest of the team. There's a significant challenge in making sure the right people surround you. That will continue to be a big challenge for any senior leader. Another challenge is creating the right atmosphere and culture. This is going to sound very simple, but believe me, it isn't. The culture needs to be very results oriented, very ethical, highly focused, open, and creative. A culture that basically wants to win together, wants to accomplish the same objectives, is energized, and does this all within the construct of being ethical, honest and forthright. Those things are very hard. You need leadership to do those kinds of things, particularly when you're trying to affect change.

Let's say you have a very goal-oriented career path and you want to scale the corporate ladder. Is it easier to move up the ladder by switching to another company or just doing a fantastic job at your current company and making sure people take notice?

I don't think it makes any difference. I think you can scale the corporate ladder both ways. At the risk of sounding controversial, I believe that people are either born natural leaders or not. I don't think people can be taught to become leaders. I think you are or you aren't. Frankly, you can see it in children. Even at very young ages, leaders emerge on the playground, on sports teams and in the classroom. And as people grow older some of them will recognize that leadership skill in themselves and will cultivate it, using it for good purposes. Interestingly, not everybody recognizes it, however, and not everybody who recognizes it, cultivates it appropriately. It is very difficult to teach people how or what it takes to motivate others to follow them because it's really more about what's inside you. You know what you're made of. It's about your inner self. You can't just teach someone to be a visionary or to be courageous.

How do you know if you're succeeding as a leader?

Again, it's all centered on people. I know I'm succeeding as a leader when I can create an esprit de corps around me. I am succeeding when there is a highly energized group of people who want to move the organization forward, a group that can work effectively together, that can remove the inhibitors that tend to distract people from accomplishing their visions. By that I mean they can disagree with each other in a constructive fashion and work cooperatively together. They can solve problems together, and they don't worry about turf. I am succeeding as a leader when my team can focus on what needs to be done for the good of the organization and the good of the company. They can actually put their own self-interests secondary to doing what's best for the company. When that kicks in, I know I've done a fabulous job.

I've heard you talk a lot about getting people to get behind a certain cause, to feel passion about what they're doing. How important is cultivating that sense of teamwork and that sense of group moving toward a common goal?

It's everything, the whole kit and caboodle. There's no way that I can do this on my own and there's no way that they can do it on their own, and so on. It is absolutely all about bringing the collective strengths, weaknesses, diverse backgrounds, and skill sets together to move the organization forward. The analogy I like to use is that it is really my role to bring together all the people who play the instruments in the orchestra. There are people who play horns, there are people who play violins, and there are people who play the piano. By themselves they sound nice, but together they make beautiful, beautiful music and the orchestra leader brings them all together and harmonizes that music so you can hear the beautiful sounds they create together.

One of the challenges for any busy executive is balancing both their professional and personal lives. How do you go about doing that?

It's something I do much better today than I did 20 years ago, because I have a better perspective on what I want out of my life. My job is not my life. For me, it's been a function of knowing who I am and what I want and understanding my priorities and having them in the right place. I would submit to you that 20 years ago my priorities were not in the right place. It was all about career, career, career. Now that I am older and wiser, it is somewhat easier today to find balance. It's really about your priorities in life, so if having children is a priority, people find a way to balance their lives in a way that allows them to spend time with their children. If being the best at your job is a priority and you don't care about anything else, then those are typically people who you'll see in the workplace at all times of the day and night. Their jobs are their hobbies. It's taken getting older, wiser, and more mature in order to lead a life that is much more in balance in terms of the priorities that I have set for myself.

Vivian Banta is an executive vice president of The Prudential Insurance Company of America and the chief executive officer of Prudential Individual Financial Services, an integrated organization with a primary focus on the protection and investment needs of retail customers. In addition to insurance and investments, this unit includes Prudential Property and Casualty Insurance Company (PRUPAC) and Prudential Bank. She also manages the retail units of Prudential Securities and Prudential Real Estate Affiliates.

Before joining Prudential, Banta took on a consulting engagement with Morgan Stanley/Dean Witter. Prior to 1997, she was an executive vice president in charge of Global Investor Services at The Chase Manhattan Corporation and its principal subsidiary, The Chase Manhattan Bank, N.A. In this capacity, she grew revenue five fold and assets under administration to over $3.5 trillion.

Banta was born and raised overseas. She lived in Lebanon, Iraq and Libya until she was eighteen years old. She attended Marymount International School in Rome, Italy and upon graduating went to the University of the Pacific in Stockton, California.

KERRI LEE SINCLAIR
Making the Most of Your Time
AgentArts
Co-Founder & Managing Director

Tell me a little bit about your background and how you got on the entrepreneurial path.

I guess I probably owe a lot of it to my parents who started a company when I was four. They're both engineers and they started as consultants - focusing on automating buildings. They put computer systems and things into buildings. From a young age I sort of had both a mother and a father who were professionals who worked for their own small business. I had the benefits of having mom and dad at home and so I saw the trials and tribulations of what they went through in that business. I actually never saw myself as somebody that would go and start a business. Actually, I still don't know what I want to be when I grow up, that's probably how I ended up where I am. I'm not scared of change and I'm willing to get my hand into anything. Over my career and in my life I've done all kinds of things. That's kind of how I've moved through my life. I went into fine arts because it was almost the direct opposite thing that I could do. After school, I started working for the provincial government doing design work. I then met an Australian and moved to Australia for a few years and while I was there my first job was to work for McKinsey and Company. I did varied roles for them. I left them to start a small property business here in Melbourne and then eventually was one of the first people to join LookSmart. I joined them very early on and spent 2 ½ years basically moving them into San Francisco and New York. It was a company that grew from 20 people, who were mostly editors to over 300 people when I left the company. I left in February of 1999 to start AgentArts with two of my business partners and basically have been managing this company since.

Tell me about the biggest challenges you've faced over the course of your career.

I still think the biggest challenge is people. I think a lot of people try to treat everybody the same. I mean it's changing as the world is developing and people are putting more priorities on different things. I still find that my biggest challenge has always been with people. They just don't act the way you expect them to. For example, at LookSmart we would have 17 people starting each day at different times. It's a really hard thing to grow a culture and grow a company when you're growing so quickly.

Everybody has some form of weaknesses. How do you approach those areas that you're not as strong in? Do you look to surround yourself with smart people in those areas?

That's probably one way, like you suggested. If you're the smartest person in the room, then you're probably in trouble. I always try to get people who know a lot more about people and those who are specialists in our areas instead of being generalists. I think one of the problems women have faced in the past is networking and I have a very strong network of women who are in business. Some vary from being 50 years older than I am to 5 years younger than I am. I go to them for advice on how to handle issues. For example, I was weak in negotiation skills when we first started looking for money. I didn't know how to go and ask for a couple million dollars in venture capital. I had never done it before, so I went and asked a couple of people who sit on boards of public companies and asked them what were some of the tactics that they used and how I could make myself stronger in those areas. You need to seek out the people who do the things that you want to do and ask them and work with them on how you can do it better. I think everything that you do you learn. I don't think anybody comes out of the box knowing how to do everything, you tend to pick it up by the people around you or by actually working very hard to develop those skills.

When you were looking for others to help you you're your negotiation skills, how did you find out who the right people were to contact and how to present yourself to them?

Again, through your networks. I'm an avid reader, whether it's on the web or television or in books or whatever. You see people either written up or you know somebody and you basically try and find a way to get in touch with them. Once you identify that person and you've gotten an introduction to that person you then make it very clear what you want from them. 99.9% of people out there will give you anything that you ask for just because what goes around comes around and they generally want to help you. If you're not clear about what you want, then it's like a danger signal to them because suddenly you're sucking up all their time and they're not getting anything for it. For example, there was a woman in Parliament I wanted to meet that my friend knew. I got in touch with her via email and was very clear with her about what I wanted. I asked if I could take her to lunch and that I'd like two hours of her time. "These are the things that I would like to discuss with you and then if you feel it's appropriate I would like to ask for another hour of your time. Approximately a month later I'd like to do a follow up and I'd like to buy you lunch again at that point." It was very clear to her what I needed from her and that she was only committing to a two hour period and perhaps a one hour period a month later. She knew she could handle that time and that I wasn't going to turn into somebody that was phoning her up every five minutes and sending her emails and letters. She wasn't going to suddenly have a terror on her hands. I also made it clear that I would buy her lunch. She said I didn't have to worry about lunch that day and that she had some time to prepare and she knew what the purpose of it was. She was able to prepare and she was able to give me a binder of information. I was able to take it away and copy what I wanted and return it to her at the next meeting. I haven't seen her in probably six months, but we've had a couple of emails. I've seen her in the press a bit. I've sort of forwarded things to her. So I have somebody out there now that knows me, but I've been able to get what I needed from her. We have a great relationship and I didn't suck her into anything she didn't want to do. I find I do the same thing. I speak to universities and high schools about how to get into IT and the business and some of the issues. A lot of people are amazed at the amount of time I'll give individual people, but it's that same sort of thing. They need to be clear about what they want from me.

Explain to me a little bit more about the right way to communicate with someone that you're looking to be your mentor. You touched on it a little bit by asking them what you want, but take me through the do's and don't when you're trying to get somebody to mentor you.

I think there are a couple of things. There's a misconception that a mentor is somebody who's older than you are, who's been there and who's done it. They basically take you under their wing and they just ooze information to you. You suddenly become a better person and I think that's a very bad perception because you could learn so much from so many people around you and you could waste so much time trying to find that perfect fit. When you approach that person they may not be interested in doing it and then you would be crushed because you've put all this effort and emotion into trying to find this person. You come into contact with people everyday and there's usually something that strikes you about them. It's either the way they dress or it's their charming personality or it's their ability to communicate an idea effectively. It's about taking each of those people and saying, "I really love the way you do that, how

69

do you do that, can you show me how you do that?" Just notice the little things around you and ask people how they do them and how they sound them out.

I guess the flip side of this is don't try to find one person that's everything you want because it'll slow you down and there are so many other things you could be learning along the way. Also, don't be afraid to ask people for their help. Most people like hearing that you like something about them, it's sort of a human emotion that we all need on some level to be liked or respected. If you go into a relationship and say, "I really like the way you do that, I don't do that well, can you tell me how you do that", 99.9% of the time you'll find that person will be blown away that you noticed it and they'll be more than happy to help you out. Don't waste their time. Try to recognize the value of what they're giving you and don't over or under do it. Don't dismiss the amount of time they're going to spend with you and say, "oh, all they did was spend an hour with me," because obviously their time is very valuable to them. Also, don't go overboard and embarrass them. Don't buy them a $700 bottle of wine or go over the top because then they feel uncomfortable. It kind of gives you that icky feeling. This person is thinking "I didn't do that much, I just helped them out a little." Also, don't be scared. So many people think "why would they want to spend time with me," or "I can't approach that person because they might say no." I guess I've always seen it as the worse case scenario is that the person says, "I'm sorry I don't have the time." That's okay and at least I know they don't have the time, but at least I went out and asked them.

How important is networking and how important has it been for you over your career?

Hard work and determination and all those things have also helped, but networking has probably gotten me to where I am. I have never given anyone my resume. I've gotten jobs based on my networks. People know me, respect me and want me to work for them. That's how I've gotten through life through those networks. I think when I worked for McKenzie and Company I learned very quickly how important networks are. McKenzie has a very strong on-line program and they have that six degrees of separation thing.

I also think networking is something that women traditionally don't do. Men have been doing it for hundreds of years. Their deals are done on golf courses, for example. They know the value of going to a networking function at 7:00 PM at night. Women recognize that networking is important, but because of their family commitments and other priorities in their life, they tend to make it a lower priority.

How important is it for women to find mentors and networks specifically with other women?

Women and men communicate differently on different levels. I think a lot of women have had some encounters of sexual harassment on some level. It's just something you deal with. However, I think it's very important to have mentors that are men also. That's actually where I've gotten most of my learning. The fact is that you understand a different side. It's like someone speaking a different language. If you could be invited into the home of someone in Zimbabwe, then you would actually understand so much more about their culture and how they live. You would be more sympathetic about how they act in their environment in the future. I think it's exactly the same with men. I worked for quite some time in Japan and it's the same there. You don't want to say "I'm looking for a tall blond woman mentor because I'm a tall blond woman." You want to say "I'm actually looking for a bunch of different types of people around me who are nothing like me because I'm going to learn a lot more from them." I think it's important to have women in your mentoring group, but not exclusively women. If you don't have variety, then I think it will be harder to succeed.

If you make a cake, you need a whole bunch of different ingredients. When looking at what's going to make you a successful individual I think you need to find all of those ingredients. Don't look at them being specifically women or specifically men or specifically Hispanic or specifically French speaking. It's just whatever you need to compliment your skills.

What is the best piece of business advice you've received along the way in your career?

It's actually a weird piece of business advice. Probably the best business advice was to exercise before or after work or at some point in the day and to discipline yourself into doing it. The gentleman who told me this is the head of one of the top Fortune 500 companies in the US. He swam every morning, at 5:00 AM. He would swim kilometers and kilometers forever and he hated it, but he said what it teaches you is discipline. It teaches you that everything is about getting up and doing it. Not forcing yourself, but disciplining yourself to be that person that swims 5k everyday. It's also such a good stress release and it also gives your mind time to switch off and think. I run 10k to work every morning and it allows me to actually plan my whole day. I'm not stressed when I get into work. I haven't had a bad commute or anything like that and I also feel good because I've gotten exercise and I'm ready to hit the day. It's also discipline that I have to get up every morning. If it's pouring rain or it's 100 degrees outside I still get up and do it. It's actually a good discipline. That's probably the best business advice because it's helped my career on so many levels and it's helped me as an individual. I think that it helps me manage my life style and things that are important to me outside of work.

For every busy individual there's always the challenge of balancing work and your personal life. How do you go about doing that?

I think it's important to understand life and that everything around you is organic and is changing. The key is trying to change with it and understand it. I suggest sitting down and figuring out exactly what you want to do. For example, "I want 5% of everyday for myself, I need 30% for the people around me, 55% is for my business and 10% is for someone else." Get the balance right on paper or in your mind about how much you need. "How much time do I need for myself everyday? Is it 5 or 10 minutes?" It's important to recognize those proportions and understand that they'll change. For example, I sit on the boards of a couple companies. When I have a board meeting I know that day is going to be 80% or 90% about that business, and the Kerri Lee time is probably going to be zero and my personal time with my family is going to be zero. Maybe the next day my personal time will be 3 hours instead of 5 minutes and I will go and have a massage or I'll go and do something that's exclusively for myself. I get very frustrated with people who are inflexible to that. For example, saying "I have to be home at 5:00 every night to be with my husband because that's really important to me." That's fine and I completely understand your lifestyle and that your husband is important to you, but some days I would rather you stay an extra hour and leave an hour earlier the next day. Having that flexibility and recognizing that life is organic and changes so much is very important. You need to recognize what you're really trying to get out of life and then allowing your schedule to change and ebb and flow based on what's happening. At the end of a period of time, say 30 days, you should have had the exact chunks of time that you wanted, but it may have all come in different blocks and different times and not every day was exactly the same.

Tell me about some of the issues that women face that are different from men, specifically with respect to succeeding in the workplace.

I think communication is probably number one. I think women are very good communicators, especially when among other women. It's been one of the strengths that a lot of women have that have done really well. It's because of their communication skills and their understanding of those sorts of things. It's obviously a limitation bursting into tears in the middle of a meeting. Women are much more open with their emotions than men and they show a lot more emotion in the way of tears, laughter, fear and everything that men don't. Generalizing, men tend to put the virtual brick face on and don't show when they're upset. They may show anger at times in meetings or at a negotiation, but they don't show all these open emotions so I think that's a challenge specifically for women. I think women tend to support people around them a lot more than they promote themselves. For example the old saying, behind every successful man is a hard working woman who has basically sacrificed herself. I don't necessarily agree with that, but I know as a woman that I will promote my team over myself. Everyone will go, Keri Lee what you've done is fantastic. I'll say, "it wasn't me, it was this person and that person and they should be recognized for doing this." I don't accept that I was a key contributor because it's more important to me that the people around me are key contributors. I think that women tend to do that.

Tell me how you set goals for yourself. I heard you say you bounced around a little bit, but I'm sure you had an idea of what you wanted to do and what would make you happy. How important have goals been for doing that and how have you set them?

I've been reading an article that talks very strongly about the subconscious mind and the goals that you actually set for yourself subconsciously. There are goals that you set for yourself consciously, but they are actually coming to the belief that subconscious goals are stronger. For example, one study showed how kids strove to get themselves to a standard above their parents and then they would stop. They couldn't figure out why all these people would stop at a level marginally better off than their parents. What they found is that these individuals had a subconscious goal to surpass their parents. For example, you don't set a goal that you want to be rich every week or every month. Therefore, you never get past that point. I strongly believe in the subconscious goals that I've set. I don't realize these goals and I don't even know what they are, so I can't tell you, but they are there.

However, I do make conscious goals, and I believe they need to be flexible. I try to do large time periods instead of an example such as the next week I'm going to lose 5 pounds. Write those goals down, put them somewhere and then pick them up when you say you're going to pick them up and see how well you've done. Sometimes you get so lost in the day-to-day minutiae that you don't actually pull your head up and see how far you've actually come. You tend to forget that you set that goal and suddenly you don't feel like you've achieved anything. Then all of a sudden when you compare it to what you've said, you've done most of these things and you are where you wanted to be.

I think it's also important to make sure your goals are across the priorities in your life. Set a goal in each area of your life, so that if 50% of your life is your work, then 50% of your goals should be around your work.

Do you think at this point in time it's easier or harder for women to advance in their careers?

I think it's harder. I think it's a classic age-old problem. If everybody thinks that there's a problem, then suddenly it's harder than when you thought there wasn't a problem. I think there's a lot more pressure on women. There are organizations out there now that are thinking, "we don't have any women on our boards or we don't have any women in our top senior management." They think, "we need to go find a woman for senior management because this is an expectation that as a leading company we have to have a woman." Then there's pressure as a woman that you suddenly have to be doing well. You have to decide that you're going to be senior management or you have to be promoted. The fact that you actually might enjoy your job and don't have grand expectations of being the CEO someday and you're quite happy in your managerial position and you don't necessarily want to be promoted can be hard for people to understand. There's this perception that if you're a woman in management, this is the time you really have to be a go-getter. You have to get out and do it, and I think that's made it harder. Again, it's that forced thinking where people are doing things because they're being told it's the right thing and it might not be the right thing for them. I think it's harder that way. I think people haven't thought that maybe some women don't want to be in those positions and maybe there are a lot women that want to do that, but there's also a lot of sacrifices those women need to make to get into those positions. It's almost a little bit harder because of the misconception that every woman in the world wants what every man in the world has. I also think it's been harder for women in the fact that it's been difficult for men as well. I'm in a very strong relationship at the moment and I have a very supportive husband, but I think it's difficult for him at times in my career when I've been more successful than he has. It's been difficult when I've been bringing in more money than he has and it's something that he's had to deal with. It's harder for women when they realize that their own success can be damaging to the people around them. It's things that they learned at school and it's the stuff nobody wants to talk about.

Tell me about some of the skills that you think are important for younger women to be learning now to give them the edge they're going to need to succeed.

I think financial skills and financial independence are important. It has been researched that one of the reasons women tend to get themselves into domestic abuse relationships is that they don't actually understand financial independence. I think that a perception still exists in places that women aren't very good at math, that boys are better at math and all this other stuff that I think is entirely false. The most important thing is that women understand smart financials, not just a balance sheet but that they understand financial independence as a woman. Financial skills are really important, as are technical skills. I encourage women to go out and code and get into software design. Things like that where it's traditionally been a man's domain. Understanding the principles of it actually helps you in problem solving. If you can understand basic coding logic you can apply it to large problems you face and break them down into smaller problems. Also, being able to use digital devices and your ability to understand the Internet and computers will make you a more sought after and successful person.

Tell me about some of the resources you've found helpful in your career. Are they books or networking events or something entirely different?

People are probably the biggest thing. I really love interacting with other individuals. Everything is a wealth of information, whether it's the taxi driver that takes you to the airport, the paper that you read at the airport, or a radio program that you listen to on the plane. It's all of those things that provide you with the information, then it's just up to you to find the parallels in your own life.

Tell me about some of the people that you admire. What are the things that impress you about them, your mentors?

I've always been impressed with people who seem cool and calm. They are always seen at the right place at the right time. I've always admired that sort of thing because I'm the opposite. I'm the goof that's tripping down the stairs and things like that. I think people who communicate effectively impress me. I can at times get rambling on about a point and I don't know when to just say my point and be quiet. I think people who speak effectively, get their points across clearly, are comfortable with their own views and don't need to justify them are very impressive. I also think people who have had a hard go of it and who have

75

not had things handed to them on a silver platter and have still succeeded are impressive. I think that is the basis of the human spirit. What makes us unique is that everyone has had our own trials and tribulations. How you've overcome those is what makes you a success, not the perception of the world and not what your success is. The people I think most highly of may not have the most highly paid jobs in the world and may not have been viewed by society as being successful, but they've overcome things that have made them either stronger as a person or have inspired others. I think those are the things that I really like about those people.

What does it take to become a leader?

It takes facilitation skills, negotiation skills, and always looking for a win-win situation. I also think being tough is important. I think there is a perception that everyone likes to be liked and there are a lot of times that you have to do things and people are not going to like you. You need to be able to get other people to realize that it is a business decision and not a personal one. As a leader you need to recognize that professionally you have to make decisions. If you have to fire someone, for example, that doesn't mean you're a bad person. It means that professionally you have to make a decision that's best for the company. A true leader will never make a decision because they're worried about hurting that person. You need to be confident and be secure enough in yourself and what you're doing to inspire people to follow you as well. People want somebody they can believe in. They want someone who is inspiring.

Tell me a little about how important it is to force yourself into new positions or new jobs in order to increase your knowledge to perform in different scenarios.

I think it's important, but it's also one of those things that on a scale of 1-10 it's probably a 6. It's more important than less important, but I think you have to be careful that you don't become too much of a generalist. People can actually do specific things specifically well and that's actually where the value will be. I think that it's important that you don't become a jack-of-all-trades and master of none. I think you need to be focused on what you want from each of the things you do and that will make your current job or your main focus better.

Can you get that experience by staying at one company for your whole career or is it more important to move around and see it from different perspectives?

If a resume came to me and the person only worked at one company I would be very hesitant in hiring them. I think you do have to move around. You don't want to be switching jobs every 12 months because that looks like you can't commit to anything. For example, working for someone like McKenzie and Company and then starting my own company, there are just so many things about working for a large company that's fantastic. I think that if I hadn't worked at McKinsey and Company, I wouldn't even understand the value of knowledge capital. If I were to leave here, I would probably go back into a larger organization because I know that there are skills there that I want to develop that only a larger organization can give me, and that would make my next small business more successful. Your bag of tricks will just keep getting bigger and bigger and your skills and your understanding of different companies will go into that bag, so to speak.

Tell me what you look for in a resume. How can you tell if someone's going to be a real up and comer, somebody that you want to have on your team, whether it's working for you or being your boss? What is it that you like to see on a resume?

It's probably unfortunate, but I mostly look at the company or companies the candidate has worked for in the past. If they've worked for a well-respected company that's known for excellence, or it has a well-respected management team, then it sounds like a pre-qualification. If you've worked for that company it means that you either have those skills or at least you have been exposed to them. I also like to see diversity. I'm not much for people who just work. I like people who have traveled, who have done different things, such as volunteer work. I think all of those different experiences, whether you're a river rafter part time or you said you work at a soup kitchen, bring something different to the table. It's about having dynamic and different people on the team. We were having a discussion here and realized that everyone but 2 individuals in the company actually speaks at least 2 or 3 languages. We didn't purposely hire those people because they spoke another language, but again it also shows that there is an underlying something about the people we were hiring. They either came from diverse backgrounds or they came from other countries. They've kind of made a go of it and they've been successful.

How do you make sure you keep learning and that you keep expanding your knowledge base?

I notice as I'm getting older I'm getting less and less interested in pushing my thinking. I'm finding that I don't want to change much and I find that at times I have to force myself to do things that normally I would have done 5 years ago without even thinking. For example, going out to an industry function on a Friday night. I start thinking, "do I not want to go because I just don't want to get out of my comfort zone, or do I not want to go for other reasons?" I think recognizing the danger is important, and I can still make the decision not to go. I'm not saying I'd force myself to go, but recognizing that five years ago you wouldn't have even thought about it because it would have been an opportunity to meet somebody is very interesting. It is important to recognize that if you start to change things, if you stop doing something that you were always doing, that's a danger signal that you're starting to slow down your learning because you're getting into a comfort zone and you're not pushing yourself out of that zone. It's the same thing when you suddenly stop reading emails or you stop reading certain types of books. For example, suddenly you're not reading technical books anymore. Instead, you're reading John Grisham novels. You've probably subconsciously made a change. By the way I'm not saying that reading John Grisham novels is not good for you, but if you're not reading those technical books anymore and you've gone into fiction books, something's happening there. You're not learning. It might be a valid change, but you need to realize those critical things. "Why am I doing this, am I doing it because I'm getting old and my comfort zone's being pushed and I'm not necessarily as open to doing these things again, or is it actually for a valid reason"? That's probably how I keep learning, just by constantly questioning why.

How do you stay on top of it from more of a business standpoint in terms of your general business knowledge and skills? Do you spend time reading specific publications? Do you target specific books? How do you know what to read since there's obviously so much out there?

What we are trying to do in the company is have lunch meetings where we focus on different areas of what's important to the business. For example, I may focus on what's happening internationally in the space of our competitors and how it differs from what we're doing. Someone else might focus on wireless devices and someone else might focus on venture capital. Basically all we do is read specific information based on those things and have a weekly lunch box meeting where we get some pizza and talk about what's changed in the wake of the space.

If you had to put your finger on two or three of the most important things for women to succeed on both a business and personal level what would they be?

Realize that you can't have it all and let the other things go. I have complete respect for women who try to do this, but women that try to be the CEO of an organization and have 17 children and a happy home and a marriage and time to themselves and do community work have something that's going to give. They're not going to be as successful as they could be if they just realized what is important to them. I guess I want to be excellent at whatever I'm doing and if/when I choose to have children I want to be successful at that. I don't want to compromise my relationship with my children because I want to be successful with my company and because I want to be a successful wife and a successful everything else. It's important to let go of everything else and realize that you can't do it all. Focus on where you have weaknesses and where you have strengths so you can impart your strengths to other people and help them become stronger at what you're strong at. Build up your weaknesses so that you become stronger in those areas. The last thing is to just have fun because if you can't get out of bed every day and enjoy what you're doing, you're not going to be very good at it.

Kerri Lee has extensive experience managing growth, technology and change in startup environments. Kerri Lee developed key hands-on knowledge in finance and administration, sales and marketing, general management, engineering, and product development for LookSmart, the most successful Australian Internet business to date. During her two years with LookSmart, Kerri Lee guided the company growth from 20 people in Melbourne, Australia to over 200 people in Melbourne, San Francisco, Los Angeles, New York and Detroit. Before LookSmart, Kerri Lee started a small business in Melbourne and previous to that, worked at the global consulting group McKinsey & Company. Kerri Lee studied a Bachelor of Fine Arts at the University of Victoria in British Columbia.

KIM FISCHER
Follow Your Dreams
AudioBasket
Co-Founder & CEO

Tell me about your background and how you ended up where you are today.

I define myself as an entrepreneur. I have always had an entrepreneurial spirit. When I was 9 or 10 I used to personalize and sell designed lunch bags to my classmates at school - at a considerable markup. After finishing my MBA at the Haas School of Business at UC Berkeley, I went to Lithuania with a program called the MBA Enterprise Corps to work on developing new businesses and privatizing old ones. While there, I founded a web design company and then worked with Motorola to develop Lithuania's most successful wireless and Internet service provider.

I've been really fortunate to have both the inspiration to start something and the dedication to see it through. As the CEO of AudioBasket, I have been able to take a great idea, work with my team, and grow it into a successful business. A little over a year ago, we were 4 people and a concept. Today, AudioBasket has over 65 employees, over $25 million in investment from companies such as Time Warner and Deutsche Telekom, customers such as AOL, partners such as NPR, CNN, and the BBC, and is the recognized leader in personalized audio news and information delivery.

What have you been known for over the course of your career?

I think I am known for my abilities as a motivating leader. As CEO of AudioBasket, I make an effort to recognize work that is well done. The most important part of any company is its human capital. As a leader, it is critical to make sure that people believe in the work they are doing and realize that they are making a contribution. I think it is very important as a CEO to recognize that the success of the company is contingent on each and every member of the team. When we close a partnership deal or a round of funding or sign up a new advertiser, the entire company shares in the celebration because the entire company is responsible for it.

I learn a lot from all of the people around me and am always open to listening to others and learning from them. Every individual I work with has taught me something. I think absorbing knowledge from your surroundings is one of the best ways to become more knowledgeable yourself.

I have a tremendous amount of energy that enables me to accomplish the multitude of tasks I face each day. I love my job, as there is always more to do. In getting things done, I focus 100% on the task at hand and accomplish goals quickly. AudioBasket is a success in part because I have built a culture that is about getting things done -effectively and efficiently.

How important has networking been over the course of your career?

Networking is a key to both business and personal success. I call it meeting people because I love to do it and networking sounds like work. Part of my job is to meet new people every day and this is something I love to do. In addition, each new person I meet seems to add to the success of AudioBasket. The individual does not have to be a potential hire, business development partner, or investor. They may just impart to me a piece of information that helps my company or they might know someone who knows someone who might be interested in joining AudioBasket. I've found that meeting and connecting with people has brought good things to me personally as well as in business.

What has been the best piece(s) of business advice you have received along the way in your career?

The best advice I've received concerns team building. As a company leader it is critical to surround yourself with people who are smarter than you are. AudioBasket's management team is made up of the most motivated, intelligent, and driven people we could find. I believe that hiring the smartest people with the most relevant experience you can find will ultimately dictate the success of your business. The cliché that A people hire A people and B people hire C people is absolutely true. I always look for A plus people and am never intimidated by people who are stronger, smarter, and more capable than I.

What has been the best piece(s) of personal advice you have received along the way in your career?

The best personal advice I have ever received was from my mother. She always taught me that I could do whatever I wanted to do. She emphasized that confidence, focus and nerve are the keys to reaching one's goals and being a successful entrepreneur. I always keep those three things in mind and I believe it has helped me to be successful. My mother is an entrepreneur and most likely the most competent person I have ever met. I am so thankful that she passed the gene along to me.

What do you find are the biggest issues women face with respect to succeeding at work and in their personal lives?

I think the biggest issue for women both at work and in our personal lives is gaining and maintaining the credibility that men are automatically granted. I do not see my capabilities as different than a man's, but there are still people out there who feel I need to work harder to prove myself. At a trade show, I was recently talking with a journalist who did not realize I was the CEO of AudioBasket. When he asked me my position, he replied, "You don't look like a CEO." Perhaps it was because I was wearing jeans, or that I weigh 110 pounds. However, I think this was definitely a gender bias related comment.

People always question me about balance in my life as well. I think this is an important question, but I don't understand why it is a gender related question. I think it is important for both men and women to have balance in their lives. If my significant other and I ever have children we plan to care for them equally, depending on the demands in our respective work lives at the time. Most of the men I know crave balance as much as the women I know.

How have you created a balance?

I think balance is subjective. I have a lot in my life: I have AudioBasket, I have a wonderful family, great friends, and a fantastic, supportive, giving, super-intelligent boyfriend. However, I do not spend the time with friends and family that I spent prior to starting AudioBasket. Luckily, these people understand my passion for my job and are still close to me despite the lack of time we spend together.

I frequent a local gym where I lift free weights, and I have a ski cabin in Tahoe, so my life is not void of activity. However, I never watch television and I don't spend much time doing what some refer to as "relaxing." This is fine with me. Some people might perceive my life as somewhat unbalanced, perhaps as somewhat crazy. However, my overflowing world of activity, both at work and play, is balance to me. I relax in different ways. When I ski or lift weights, my mind is completely free - for me, this is a form of meditation and the ultimate relaxation.

In the last couple of years has it become harder or easier for women as a group to advance in their careers?

Eleven years ago, when I started my first business, and went out to raise funding, investors always turned to my male business partner to ask the questions. I was the one who wrote the business plan and knew the answers cold, but even if I did the entire presentation, investors would then turn and ask questions of my partner.

Today, I have six Vice Presidents working for me, all men, and a few over ten years older than I. However, now when we go to present to Venture Capitalists, the questions are all directed back to me. They know I am in charge and look to me for the answers where they used to look to my male business partner. Only once in the tens of venture presentations we gave did the investors assume that one of my VP's was actually the CEO. Despite that incident, I am feeling there is progress in the investment community regarding the perception of women.

I think slowly, but surely, it is becoming easier for women to advance in their careers.

What advice would you have for women trying to succeed in the business world?

In order to succeed in the business world, women need education, courage, and conviction. Evaluate your resources and ask for advice. Arm yourself with as much knowledge as possible about the path you pursue. Also, look for the opportunity in every risk and really muscle up and be courageous.

If you are starting your own business, you will inevitably face a lot of resistance along the way. For example, raising money will probably be the single most frustrating and humbling thing you'll do.
- Some very smart, successful people will say "no."
- Some won't like the market.
- Some won't like the team.
- Some won't believe you can do the job.
- Some will tell you they don't want to invest, but won't tell you why.
- Try not to be discouraged. It's not a personal rejection.

This is the kind of experience that will require you to be courageous, believe in what you are doing and move on from rejection. AudioBasket received plenty of rejections when we were initially looking for financing. Now that we are successful, investors frequently call me asking if they can invest. You need to have strength, courage and flexibility to move from the stage where you are "begging for money" to the stage where people will be begging you to take their money.

How important are technology skills and having an understanding about the "Internet economy"?

At AudioBasket, when we want to test out products to ensure that they will be understood by technologically unsavvy users, I am the guinea pig of choice. It helps to understand markets and how technology affects the economy. It is important to understand the process of developing technology. However, to be a CEO, it is not important to be a technologist.

An interesting business difference between the new economy and the old is how quickly you need to react. When I was involved in my first startup, a fitness center, my competition was only the other fitness centers within five miles of my own. If new competition was entering the market, I knew well in advance - I could see them building the facility.

In the Internet economy, competition can come from anywhere and it can happen without warning. In addition, your competitors will know about absolutely everything you do by visiting your website, reading your press releases online, etc. This change has created a tremendous shift in the way people need to do business today. Creating sustainable barriers to entry for your company is more important than ever. You need to make sure that you have something very difficult for a competitor to copy. You need to be nimble and able to react quickly. If a competitor enters your market space, you need to decide what to do and do it quickly - whether it is to stand strong, or to lower your prices, alter your target market, emphasize new product features, launch a new product, etc.

This dynamic is very important to understand and requires two skills. First, an understanding of game theory. It is important to always consider what your competition might do and how you would react if they did it. Also, to consider how your competition might react to a change you make, and what your counter-move will be. Thinking through these scenarios enables companies to be nimble and able to react quickly when a competitive move is made. In addition, an ability to scour the environment, assess it's effect on your business, and react quickly has become a key to success in business.

What are some good resources for women (books/networking groups/mentoring, etc.)?

The wealth of resources available for women in business in the United States is tremendous. These resources and networks provide women a definite edge where they might otherwise not have one. I am actively involved in a few such groups. In addition, I have found a wonderful network through interaction with other woman CEO's. Because there are so few of us, an informal support network exists.

Here are some great networking groups for women:

FWE - "The Forum for Women Entrepreneurs" - Most notably, this group puts on a venture conference called "SpringBoard" in many different US cities throughout the year. SpringBoard is a very selective venture conference that accepts applications from woman run companies who want to present their businesses to a large group of investors. Because the companies are pre-screened and a few are selected out of hundreds of applications, the investors that come to these conferences know they are seeing a select group of potentially very successful companies. After presenting at SpringBoard 2000, I made contacts that enabled me to raise over $20 Million for AudioBasket from investors such as Time Warner and Deutsche Telekom. Last year only 4% of venture capital in the US went to women run companies. The FWE and SpringBoard are working to change that.

WTC - "The Women's Technology Cluster" - This is an incubator in San Francisco for women led technology companies. AudioBasket started our business here and it was wonderful to have an instant network of other professional, successful women to work with, interact with, and share our experiences with.

WITI - "Women in Technology International"

Gracenet - this is a Bay Area organization for business women.

Do leaders have to make sacrifices to have a successful career?

It is important to understand yourself and your goals. I wouldn't say you need to make sacrifices for a successful career, but you most definitely need to make trade-offs. You need to decide what trade-offs are acceptable to you. It is impossible to be the stereotypical "superwoman" - all-consuming job, happy family, balanced life. However, if one of your main goals is to have a successful career, it is important to decide what trade-offs are acceptable. If you want to be a super mom and have a career, you can still have a successful career. However, you may want to choose a career that enables you to work flexible hours from home. My best friend has two young children and she has a successful recruiting company that she runs out of her garage. She has flexible hours that enable her to run her business and take care of her children. Her business would most likely grow beyond her garage if she made that choice, but she doesn't need to and is happy being able to have a small business and a happy family. Her business is not a success in that it generates hundreds of millions of dollars, however it is a success in that it generates enough to be a profitable, sustainable business while providing her both enough income and time to support her family well. She has made trade-offs that give her a satisfied life.

I have done the same. I used to work out six days a week, now it is two. I used to go out three or four nights a week with friends, now it is one or two. I spend a lot of time working with my team at AudioBasket and this is time that I don't have to do other things. However, I adore working with my team, and making AudioBasket a success brings me great satisfaction. It is important to me that there are other aspects to my life, but my company requires me to limit some of these other aspects. This is a conscious trade-off that I am satisfied with. However, it is a trade-off.

Is there any way to have children and still be on an "executive track?" How do you go about doing this?

I am 32, and don't yet have children. However, my mother is a true inspiration to women who want both a successful career and a family. My mother had four children in ten years and was a stay at home mom for twenty-two years. Prior to this, she was a programmer at IBM. After my youngest sister entered high school, my mother decided to re-enter the work force in the market research industry. She took a few courses at a local college and found a job in a small company with two other women. Three times she changed companies, eventually moving to the top of her industry as a Project Director for The Gartner Group. She did this after five years of work - after 22 years as a full time mom. After ten years, she decided she had accomplished a successful career and wondered what to do next. She is currently works with startup companies as a freelance market research professional.

You have to have a lot of guts and a lot of determination to accomplish what my mother did after so many years out of the work force. However, if you have the right attitude and ability to learn, I think today's workforce enables women to enter and leave and re-enter the workforce without losing much momentum.

I've worked in the fitness industry, multimedia, wireless, Internet, and retail over the last ten years and have become an expert in each industry. Information is so easily available today, that you can re-enter the workforce after time off and be able to come up to speed quickly. The key is to gain broad skills that can transcend both time and industry. This is easier than one might believe. I graduated from my MBA program in 1994 - right before the Internet became something that that people outside academia knew about. After I graduated, I noticed my schools curriculum changing - there were new classes that had not been available to me: e-commerce, new venture finance, Internet marketing, etc. In 1998, I decided I should take a refresher course to ensure that my skills were still relevant. I took an online MBA course offered by The Wharton School (my undergraduate alma matter) in Entrepreneurship. I was amazed to discover that the course included Porter Analysis and other readings and lessons that I had learned not only in business school in 1992, but also in college, in 1986. The basics of marketing, finance, accounting, have not changed. The economy has changed, the nature of competition has changed, and there are always new accounting rules. However, I learned that my basic business skills were still exactly the skills that were required in the new economy.

What sort of opportunities does the "Internet Economy" present for women specifically?

Women have not traditionally entered the work force as regularly as men, especially prior to the last twenty years. Therefore, there are many fewer women in the workforce who have twenty plus years of high-level work experience. The Internet, or any new industry, provides an opportunity for women in that no one has worked extensively in the Internet industry for over six years.

I've found this to be true in the wireless industry as well. From 1995 through to 1999, I worked in wireless. In addition, AudioBasket's personalized news and information service is also provided to wireless carriers to deliver their customers the news they want to here, wherever they are. I now find myself being considered an "expert" and an "old-timer" in this industry because I have been involved in it for just five years. Although wireless has been around for a long time - wireless networks were being launched in the early 1980's in the US - my five years still makes me a guru in this field.

Technological change is occurring more quickly than it has in the past. This provides women the opportunity to be at the forefront of industries, even though they may not have been in the workforce as long as men.

How can you keep learning?

It is really important to follow industry research. I find it is very important to take the time to read all of those publications to which I subscribe - and there are many. Also, I think it is important to not just read material that focuses on your industry. I also read things that have nothing to do with my job, not just to keep myself well rounded, but because there are other things I care about. I read the Economist, because I care what is happening in the world. I read the Baltic Times, as I am curious as to the progress being made in the region I worked for three years. I currently fly to New York almost every week. I don't work on airplanes unless absolutely necessary. I usually complete two books each trip and this helps me feel my life has balance.

I also love learning languages. In my last position, as Director of Strategic Business at a wireless startup, I had an hour commute in each direction. I also frequently traveled internationally for my job. I had a whole serious of tapes from Portuguese to Japanese that I would listen to and practice on my way to and from work. This was not only personally satisfying to me, but made my visits to these countries much more understandable and enjoyable.

How important is it to force yourself into new positions and force yourself to learn new things?

I think it depends on how much you feel like you are "forcing" yourself. There is no reason to suffer - if doing new things is painful to you, perhaps you should accept your life as it is, as long as you can be happy with that. I think, however, that most people enjoy self-improvement and learning new things. It is important to stay somewhat within your comfort zone, however. If you are terrified of speaking in front of people, you can try and overcome this through training and by presenting to increasingly large audiences. However, you may also want to consider a career that takes more advantages of your strengths, whether they are writing skills, programming, analysis, or something else.

I love to try new things, but I also know there are areas in which I can excel and areas where I have little hope of success. I am a lousy detail person and have no sense of direction - I could try and improve these skills, but I prefer to focus on improving skills I am already good at, such as public speaking, so that I can excel at these. Despite the title of this book you can't really "have it all." No one is good at everything. In a sense you can have it all by working together with people whose skills compliment your own. At AudioBasket, this is what I have done. Brian Fisher, my brother and AudioBasket's CTO, has exactly the skills I lack. He is a technical genius, a perfectionist, and a great manager, who also has a solid business sense and understanding of the market. Whereas my focus at AudioBasket is external - fund raising, partnering, and PR. Because of his intelligence and well-rounded knowledge, combined with his attention to detail, I know that all the right decisions are being made for the company, even if I am on the road.

What are the main things that impress you about people that work for you?

I am really impressed by my employees' dedication to AudioBasket. Everyone who works for AudioBasket really believes in the technology and in the business model. We are providing an incredible technology that allows the customization of news and information and everyone here is really fired up about that. It is that energy and conviction that has made AudioBasket the leader in our space.

Is it easier to become a leader at one company?

I think this depends so completely on what that company is and what the opportunities for success are at that company. Many people have found success in the last fifteen years by moving from company to company. I moderated a panel recently at the "Women In Leadership" conference at UC Berkeley. The panel was about women in media. I noted that all the women worked in "new media" where I had expected to be moderating a panel of executives from the top traditional media companies. I asked the panelists what their decision criteria were for choosing the companies they work at. They all answered that "attitude towards women" was one of the top criteria for their choice. They had all come from old media, but felt that at a certain level, there was a barrier to growth opportunities. For these women, moving to new companies was important for their career growth. However, now that they have found companies they feel they can prosper in, most of them planned to stay put.

AudioBasket's recruiting manager recently told me that having a woman CEO was a top selling point to job candidates, both male and female.

How important is networking?

Networking is a huge key to success - although as I mentioned earlier, I like to call this "meeting people." For me, this skill was developed partly through always moving a lot. My whole life, I have moved to a new place every three to five years. I've lived on the East Coast, in California, in France, and in Lithuania. Each time I move I am required to create a new network of both friends and associates. Perhaps this is a skill I have developed out of both need and practice.

How important do you think it is to give back to your community?

It is very difficult to run a business and contribute time to the community as well. However, I think it is very important to be socially responsible and to give something back. At AudioBasket we found a way to do this through the Women's Technology Cluster. When you join the Cluster, you provide them with 2% of the equity in your company. Upon a liquidity event (acquisition or IPO), the cash that results from this 2% is given back to the community. It is up to the CEO's of the Women's Technology Cluster to determine how and where this money will be spent. This provides an incredibly unique opportunity to startup companies. When you are starting a company you tend to have both very little time and very little money - therefore making it difficult to contribute in any way. This 2% enabled AudioBasket to give back to the community at a time when the founders had both no time and no money of our own.

One of the reasons I went to work in Lithuania, was to do something charitable through the use of my time and my skills. The MBA Enterprise Corps enabled me to work with companies in this developing country and to, in a small way, contribute to the countries growth. My goal is to use the money that will be generated through AudioBasket's 2% to create a "Women's Technology Cluster" in Lithuania. To give ambitious entrepreneurs in a country where it is much more difficult to gather the resources required to start a business, the opportunity to accomplish their dreams and contribute to the countries progress.

What advice would you give a startup?

You need a few main things:

1)   A great idea. I am not an idea person, but one of the main reasons I joined the AudioBasket team was because our Marketing VP, Andrew Edelson, came to me with a great idea. The concept for AudioBasket was completely

unique and there was a clear market need - this is rare to find. Not only was the idea important to me, but it is the idea that infects our investors, business partners, and employees with enthusiasm. The idea should also be unique. It is okay to have competition, all good ideas do, but something about the concept should be different enough from the competition that you will sustain your success despite them. You need to have sustainable barriers to entry. For example, one of the reasons I was so attracted to AudioBasket is that it has created a lot of new technology. Our 30 engineers have created patent pending technology that makes it difficult for other companies to easily provide what we are providing to the market.

2)   A good business model. A cool product is not a business if you can't make money off of it. Before deciding to start a company, make sure that your concept is one that will make money, lots of money, and understand how this will happen. Who is the market? How big is it? How much will they buy? How much will they pay?

3)   A strong management team. Starting a company on your own is tough to do. I started AudioBasket with three partners and quickly brought in two other key managers. I don't know how I would have done it without them.

4)   A solid business plan that explains all of the above: your product, business model, and management team. AudioBasket had the advantage of my prior experience creating business plans - not just for my own businesses, but also as a consultant for other businesses. Being able to communicate your business through a solid business plan is important. There are great books out there that can help - such as "Business Planning" by Ernst and Young, as well as software packages.

5)   Money. Raising money is very important to the success of a startup. In my experience raising $25 million for AudioBasket, I learned quite a few things. My first piece of advice in this arena is to suggest planning to raise capital at least six months before your company actually needs it. Also, I strongly suggest holding off on any kind of celebration until the check has cleared.

While I was out raising money, I was lucky to have a management team in place that could allow me to be out pounding the pavement, presenting at venture forums, talking to press and analysts and raising capital. I was also fortunate to have a VP of Finance who could crunch lots of numbers at a moment's notice.

I have also learned very quickly that the key to raising enthusiasm about your business is to be enthusiastic about it yourself. This means not only knowing how to talk about your business but also knowing your audience. Understand who you are presenting your business model to and identify the key elements that will interest them the most. This may be different, for example, for a venture capitalist who will be interested mainly in optimizing their return on investment than for a strategic investor who will want your business to fit in with an aspect of their own.

How do you become an executive/C-level employee?

In order to become a good CEO, I think it is really important to have a vision and a clear understanding of the steps it takes to make that vision a reality. It is also critical to earn the trust of those around you. Part of earning that trust involves communicating to your team, keeping them involved in the decision-making processes and getting their input on the company's strategy. A unified and well-informed management team and board of directors are essential to the success of a business.

I personally never planned to become a CEO. For me, the goal has always been to build things, to make a difference, and to enjoy myself while doing so. It is not important to me whether my title is CEO or Marketing Associate, as long as I can achieve and contribute to these goals.

What are the three most important things it takes to succeed on both a business and personal level in the 21st century?

1.   Be not afraid - The most important ingredient for success in the 21st century really is the ability to take the risk required to pursue your dreams. Looking back on your life the only risk you will ever regret is the one you did not take. Starting a business, traveling the world, fully giving yourself to those you love, can be scary. But it is scarier to never know whether or not your dreams can be accomplished. And if you put your mind to it, they most likely can be.

2.   Listen - When I talk to most people I feel like they are just waiting for me to finish talking so that they can say something. Listening not only shows a respect and care for those around you, but it also makes you a better person. Absorb knowledge from those around you. Share your experience with them, but also listen to theirs.

3.   Have a life - I strongly believe that there is more to life than work. I have really made a point of insuring that AudioBasket's corporate culture allows for more than work. I believe that people should work hard and play hard - but not necessarily within the same four walls. Unlike a lot of startups, AudioBasket doesn't have any foosball tables or beanbag chairs. We do have ergonomic

workstations and a subsidized gym membership. I think that our employees are more creative because they have the chance to experience life outside of work. That makes them happier about working at the company.

Kim Fisher has worked for over ten years with entrepreneurial ventures. Most recently, she was Director of Strategic Business for Synacom Technology, Inc., a wireless telecommunications software company funded by Cisco Systems. Prior to working at Synacom, Kim was Senior Marketing Manager in Motorola's International Joint Venture division. She has worked in the Internet industry, both as the Marketing Manager for an Internet Service Provider and as the co-founder of one of Lithuania's first Web page design companies. Kim has an MBA from the University of California at Berkeley, Haas School of Business, where she was a Graduate Student Instructor for Entrepreneurship as well as the winner of the Price Fellowship for Entrepreneurial Promise. She also has a BS in Economics from the Wharton School of Business and two patents pending in the field of wireless telecommunications software.

KRISHNA SUBRAMANIAN
Keep Learning
Kovair
CEO

Tell me how you ended up where you are today.

Prior to this I was working at Sun Microsystems where I was working on their new products. I was working fairly closely with some of our key customers and partners at Sun trying to understand what their needs were and see how we could better align our products to meet those customers' needs. In that role I realized how complex business-to-business relationships can get. So that's when I was thinking, "Why can't we build a technology infrastructure to manage these high-end, strategic business-to-business relationships?" I looked at what it would take if Sun had to build this in-house and realized it would be a multi-million dollar investment because it's a fairly complex system. I was telling my co-founder about all my problems and he thought of a technology infrastructure that we could use to address this issue. So together we left and started Kovair.

What do you enjoy most about where you are today?

I just love what I'm doing because I feel strongly about this problem that we're solving. I enjoy all the customer interaction I have and I can make a real difference in the market. I truly want this to be a dominant solution for major companies, and it's very rewarding to actually put this out in the field. We're at the point where we're deploying to major customers, they're seeing results from it and it's a very rewarding experience overall.

What attributes have helped you through your career to get you where you are today?

I'd say the most important thing is probably the passion I have for the work I do. It's enabled me to give the job everything I have without any worry about the outcome or the results. You get better results when you put more into something. Another thing I would say is the ability to make quick decisions has been very important. It's very hard, especially in a startup environment. You often don't have all the information at your fingertips. Everything is new and nobody has thought of this before so there's no market data to say this is what we need to be doing. A lot of times you've got to make decisions very, very quickly and stick with those decisions in order to move fast. Fortunately I'm a pretty fast decision maker, and that's been extremely helpful.

What led you to focus on technology and work for Sun and later to start Kovair?

It's something I liked from childhood. I grew up partly in India and then in West Africa, and there I got introduced to computers. Believe it or not I was using punch cards for my class project, and I enjoyed it. I liked that it was one of those fields that had so many applications in so many industries. For example, I did my master's at the University of Illinois, and there we were using massive parallel computer programs to trace the human genome. It's just such a fascinating thing. There are so many different combinations that you have to go through to track down the genetic sequences and you really need computers to help you with that. A human just can't do those things, and I guess that's the aspect of technology that appeals to me the most. I'm not good at just looking to technology for technology's sake but more at the applications of technology.

What has surprised you the most about your career as it's developed?

I don't know if anything has really surprised me. Making the jump to start this company is something that's surprising just because I had not really thought of necessarily doing this. I was enjoying my work at Sun, and I wasn't really actively thinking I would leave and do a startup. So I guess that would be the biggest surprise.

What's been the best piece of business advice that you've received?

I've received so much good advice. Probably the best piece of advice I've received was early on when I was looking to leave Sun to start this company. Someone said, "Make sure you're really, really convinced about what you're going to do, because it's going to be a lot of ups and a lot of downs and initially a lot more downs than ups."

I also received some good advice on how to hire, and to always look for the best. That's another one that's hard early on. You don't have much money and nobody knows who you are, but someone told me, "Don't settle for second best, always look for the best and you can motivate the best to join you."

What are the biggest issues you've faced in trying to succeed in a demanding job and trying to have a personal life?

I don't have any children so it's not as difficult as it might be for some people who are trying to juggle kids and a work life. I think the biggest challenge is to learn to balance life, because you can get caught up in it and be working all day, night, and weekends. Taking time out to go do something else is very important because it actually refreshes you. It gives you a fresh perspective. You can never work at 100 percent efficiency working all the time.

How important has setting goals been in your career?

I probably look at it differently. I'm not one who says in three years this is where I want to be and then I start climbing toward that. I'm very much a gut-based person. I go with my instincts, and then as I go through things I get new ideas of where I can go next. So for me the answer is the goals aren't as important.

How do you not get overloaded with too many things?

I think that's hard. I think you have to prioritize, and that's always very hard in life. First of all, I think you can't ever just do one thing, because you play different roles in your life and have different responsibilities. You have to know how to juggle a few things as long as it's not too many. I usually try to pick one thing as my top priority at any point. Right now this company is my top priority and everything else is a second priority. It helps me in making decisions along the way.

In the past couple of years do you think it's become harder or easier for women to advance in their careers?

I think it has been easier up to a point. I think that there has been a tremendous change in the role of women in technology, and I'm extremely excited about that. While I was at Sun I was involved with an organization called Women in Technology International, which is an incredible organization promoting and helping women, especially in technical roles. You see a big change in corporate America, the fact that you have people like Carly leading HP and top-ranked executives even in the Fortune 500 companies. I think it's an encouraging sign. Things have opened up a lot for women, but having said that I think there's also more we can do. We have a lot of organizations that are trying to do just that.

97

For example, I'm on the board of an association called The Forum for Women Entrepreneurs, and our goal is to be a support network for women trying to start their own companies and women in senior-level positions in the bigger companies. We take on a mentoring role and provide a network that these women can access.

How important has the Internet been for providing new opportunities for women?

I think the Internet and software in general have been an incredible force in providing opportunities for women in a couple of ways. First of all, they've really lowered the barrier to access and the barriers to start a company. You can start a company with just a few people and a couple of laptops, and you can work from pretty much anywhere, so it's made it a lot easier for women who have lifestyle restrictions and can't always be in the office. Second, I think the Internet has lowered the gender bias to an extent because it's a job that you don't need manual labor to do. It's something that if you're smart and you understand it, you can come in and do the job.

Are there any specific impediments that you've seen that only women must overcome in your industry?

I think the biggest is getting access to a network. Because there have been fewer women in the workplace over time, there have been fewer women in senior management positions, so the network that they have is not very extensive. That's why associations like FWE are forming to provide women access to a wider network. As a woman you can always network with men too, it's not an exclusive thing, but it does help when you have somebody else you can relate to.

Did you have a mentor who helped you?

I've had a lot of mentors, I haven't just had one. A lot of people have helped me for a lot of different reasons, from my mangers at Sun to PR people to even CEO's of other companies.

Who have you come across in your career that you've admired?

Again, it's not any one person. There have been quite a few people who have done an incredible job that I have admired. For example, if I look at our high-tech market, companies like Apple and Sun, their management is pretty incredible and so is the direction in which they've taken their companies. The new economy companies like Ariba that have a powerful vision and executed on it I admire as well.

Are there any women who you've come across in your career that you've admired?

I don't know Carly from HP personally, but reading about her and some of the bold moves she's making makes me admire her a lot. I have encountered other women you may not know about in senior management positions. They're not celebrity women, but they're people like vice presidents at companies like Sun that have been very, very strong.

What skills really impress you?

I think leadership skills are the number one thing I admire in these people. They have a strong vision where they want to take something, and they're able to lead a group of people to get to that point. They're articulate in what they want to do and passionate and driven about how they want to get there. In some, especially with women, their management style is very unique. A lot of them are more team-oriented, not very individual-focused, and I think this is a medium that really helps women in management. Between the Internet and the new economy, the emphasis is on teamwork. No one person can pull these companies through. You've got to have a group of people working together, building, putting their creative thoughts together and building something. And from what I've seen in my career, women managers generally tend to be very team-oriented people, bringing out the individual strengths of different people in an organization.

What have been the most difficult choices you've had to make in your career?

I've not really had difficult choices because I made most of the choices because I wanted to make them. Probably some of the big ones were where I switched directions. For example, when I first went out of the technical role into doing more customer involvement, that was something I had to think about because it was a change in my career direction. The second thing was when I left Sun to start this company. That was a big decision, but I wouldn't say it was a difficult decision.

What skills should women be learning to excel in the future?

There are a couple of things. First, women should not be afraid to make bold moves. I think that a lot of times it's hard because it's early on and there's not that many women in these positions. Almost everybody who's making a move in a way is a pioneer, so I would encourage women not to be afraid to make that move, to think of themselves as leaders and to be assertive in what they're saying. If they have a strong vision and a feeling for something, go and execute on that. Because historically women have not been in that many senior positions, we may need more training and help in traditional management approaches or organization building. Though they have a good intuitive sense of it, it doesn't hurt to have traditional knowledge around it.

Do you think that technology skills are becoming more important for women to learn?

Yes, absolutely, that's a big portion. In fact, it is important for girls in high school to learn even before they become women. It's becoming increasingly important to have a strong technology background in almost any field that you're in. One of the things that we're trying to do is to encourage girls in high schools to learn more about technology and to become comfortable and familiar with technology. Then as they grow and advance in their careers, they have that solid background. Technology skills are very important, and that's something women traditionally have shied away from.

What are some good resources for women?

I think the networking groups are excellent. I mentioned Women In Technology International and Forum for Women Entrepreneurs. WITI is a national organization and started out in the Silicon Valley, but it's expanding now. There are a lot of these entrepreneurial associations, and if you're interested in entrepreneurship, I would say those are good resources.

Do you feel that leaders in your industry have to make sacrifices in order to have a successful career?

I think life is full of choices and you always can make whatever choices you want to make, so I don't think of anything as a sacrifice. You're picking your priorities. Having said that, I think it is a competitive environment and a very fast-paced environment, especially in technology. As a result, it's very intense and it's not for everyone. It's a choice you have to make when you're coming into this field, especially if you want to become a leader in this field.

How did you become a leader in this field? How did you evolve into your position?

For me it happened more because I wanted to start this company and because there was a problem I wanted to solve. I wanted to build a solution that addressed the needs of companies in the market, so it evolved. It wasn't a conscious decision that I made saying that I wanted to become a leader.

What advice would you give to a new startup?

Early on make sure you validate your concept. There's a lot of good ideas out there, and a lot of ideas might not make it, not because they're not good ideas but because either the market isn't ready for the idea or the idea isn't sustainable over time. So early on, I think it's extremely important for a company to get as much real customer feedback and real market validation as possible. I think when you start a company all you have is the idea, and you tend to be very protective of it. Often it's your own idea, so you tend to think the world of it, but it's important to make it a little more objective and run the idea by a few people, potential customers, and to get feedback because it's going to help you define the idea.

How important is it to continue learning through your career?

I cannot emphasize the importance of it enough, because things are changing all the time. If you really want to grow in your career, everyday you've got to be learning something new. That's what's going to help you advance.

How important is it to put yourself in new positions in a company?

A lot depends on what you want to do in your career. For example, I know a lot of people who are software engineers, they've been software engineers all their life, and that's what they enjoy. If you tell them to learn a lot of other things, I don't think they're going to be happy with that. There are other people who really want to have a diversified experience and grow into other positions, and they really enjoy exposure to different things. Success in a career is very individualized.

Do you think it's easier to become a leader by branching out and starting your own business?

I think gender plays a little bit of a role there too. First of all, a leader is not just somebody who has the title of a leader. In any group, even if they're all peers, you can spot the leader. It's a skill and an inherent talent. You can hone your leadership skills anywhere. It doesn't have to be for a big company. But if you're looking for growth in your career and to move into management positions, I do think it's easier in a startup because a startup is always growing, and your contributions are much more visible and there's a lot more opportunity.

What are the most important things it takes to succeed in business?

To succeed in business, the most important things are to have a good understanding of what you want to succeed in, to actually be focused on what success means to you and to figure out how you can build your career around that. A lot of times people are unhappy in their jobs or they're not growing in their jobs, but they don't recognize that. If you know what you want, it becomes a lot easier because you recognize the red alarms faster and you can get other people to help you. You can always ask your manager and your peers for their input. Every company wants its people to succeed, so that is a support system that you can leverage.

Krishna Subramanian co-founded Kovair to provide a collaborative solution for companies, enabling them to coordinate their relationships with key customers. Prior to Kovair, Krishna was at Sun Microsystems where she was instrumental in designing the strategy that made Java a platform for business users. She also led new product development for Sun's Java Studio, dubbed "Java for the masses." Krishna was then appointed the Lead for the product Sun.Net, which was sold to Sun's major networking clients, including Lucent Technologies.

Krishna was recognized by Women in Technology International as an Outstanding Technical Woman, 1996. She holds five patents from her work at Sun, and has published numerous papers. Krishna earned her Masters in Computer Science from the University of Illinois, Urbana-Champaign, and her Bachelors degree in Computer Science and Business Administration from Angelo State University, Texas.

MONA LISA WALLACE
Keep Perspective
RealEco.com
CEO

Tell me about your background and how you ended up where you are today.

I am an attorney by trade, with a passion for both technology and social activism. Balancing a commitment to one's values and paying back student loans walks a narrow tightrope in any career. The legal and financial industries provide exceptional challenges for a woman with social returns at heart. In a world that equates the bottom line with personal value, it was tremendously challenging to earn the support of the venture capital community. Having focused on environmentally conscious business practice in the early part of my career, I discovered that the Internet's power to redistribute information and facilitate supply chain management was vastly underutilized in the eco business industry.

What do you enjoy most about what you're doing today?
In addition to the intellectual challenge and the opportunity to meet a lot of different people, running this business gives me the potential to make a difference in the world.

What do you think are your best attributes that have helped you through the course of your career?

Tenacity and creativity. I became pregnant during the closing of my first round of funding. Perhaps not so coincidentally, several of my investors backed out soon after I announced my happy news. Despite being pregnant and being able to function on about half of the money that we had initially planned on having, I managed to pull everything together, launch and build the company anyway.

103

How did you develop these skills? How did you develop your tenacity?

My mother always told me I could do anything I set my mind to. She also taught me to finish what I start. It could also be called stubbornness, right?

What has surprised you the most about your career as it has developed?

I think what has surprised me the most has been that I never really expected so many people in business to share a deep commitment to the environment and be so willing to help. It really took me by surprise how incredibly generous and helpful people in the business world have been. Doing good business is not just about a financial return on investment, the social return on investment is just as important.

What do you feel is the best piece of business advice you've received along the way in your career?

I think it was probably to keep things in perspective. Business goes up and down. There are pretty hard times and there are great times and keeping it in perspective is important. You need to remember that you've got your family and your outside life Those things are what you'll remember 10 years from now, not necessarily the deal that did or did not go through. The best advice I've received is to maintain the long-term perspective about life in general.

What are the biggest issues that you've faced with respect to succeeding at a demanding job and also having a personal life?

I think a lot of that is the expectations of the industry. I've had venture capitalists call me on Saturday afternoon to have business conversations. One caller got through to me on my cell phone the day after I got home from having my baby. When I described my situation, he asked, "Should I call back tomorrow?" I think the expectation now is that we'll be working 24 hours a day, no matter what.

How do you overcome this and create a balance?

Balancing work and the rest of your reality is a continual process. I relocated my office to a space that was closer to my home. I set up an office space in my home as well. Since we often have business meetings in the wee hours of the morning, an equipped home office is a necessity. It's a cozier environment for my staff and more convenient for my work life. It IS possible to be comfortable while working. After a late night, I will sometimes take the afternoon off.

How important are setting goals?

It is almost as important as being flexible about those goals. Keeping the distinction between goals and objectives is critical. For example, it is an objective to launch the site by January 2. If your quality is not up to par on January 2, then it just might turn out that you are better off waiting before creating a PR disaster. The launch by January 2 is just an objective, your actual goal is to successfully launch your site.

How important has the Internet economy been for providing opportunities for women?

The Internet has opened up new windows of opportunity for everyone. With organizations such as the Women's Technology Cluster and the Forum for Women Entrepreneurs, women finally have the opportunity to network with each other for capital access. Making use of the technological opportunities provided by the Internet economy requires access to capital as well as insight. Money, ability and insight constitute three necessary ingredients in achieving the potential offered by opportunity. It is access to capital that is the highest hurdle for most women entrepreneurs.

Why do you think so little venture capital has been invested in women run companies and do you think it's fair?

Whoever said business was fair? It's not always an intentional sexist system, sometimes it is just a de-facto one. If you're a 30-year-old male CEO and you say guess what, my wife's pregnant or my partner and I are adopting, the correct response is, "Congratulations." But if you're a women and you say, "Good news, I'm having a baby," your reaction is, "Oh my God, what's going to happen to the company?" There's a physiological difference there, but what greatly impedes the company's ability to get funding is outside perceptions. I was just as capable, if not more determined during my pregnancy. The problem was how I was perceived, not in my ability. Men take paternity leave too.

In the last couple of years has it become harder or easier for women as a group to advance in their careers?

It has become easier as the networking progresses. But, I certainly wouldn't call it easy!

Are there any other specific impediments than physiological that women must overcome in the industry in order to succeed?

I just want to clarify that physiological difference. I was fine during my pregnancy. I was working just fine. My problem was not so much that I couldn't do the work during my leave. The time it usually takes to have a baby is just a few weeks. If you're a man, you could throw out your back in a skiing accident and miss that many days. Anything like that could happen to put you out of commission for a few weeks. I just want to clarify that a lot of the physiological differences are simply perceptions of others. As a mother, I think I'm a much more aggressive and serious a business person.

How did you overcome these impediments?

Again, just networking among women and building alliances with other women and with enlightened men.

Did you have a mentor that helped direct you in your career?

Absolutely fabulous mentors: Julie Stein, Margarita Quihuis, Cate Muther, Rob Kruger and Jim Robbins. Each and every one of them is fabulously successful and both a parent as well as in business.

What are the skills that women should be learning right now in order to be successful?

Leadership skills - being able to project manage and work with a variety of different talents to accomplish a single goal is very important. Technology skills are also very important. It's one thing to do business on the Web as far as e-commerce, but if you're trying to utilize technology to accomplish some business practice, then you have to understand your technology and understand what it's potential is. You have to understand what's out there, what the different options are. To manage "techies" you need to understand what's going on to communicate and to deserve their respect.

What do you feel are some good resources for women, like mentoring groups that you talked about?

I would recommend FWE and the Women's Technology Cluster. I think the important thing is to deal with women that you can meet with in person. I think that it really helps to be physically interacting. National organizations are great, but it's also good to get with your local NOW organization (National Organization of Women) as well.

How important is it to keep learning?

Just read every day. I take a certain amount of time every day to read. I read on the web and I read the New York Times. I read slashdot.org for my sanity.

How important is it to put yourself in new positions where you can learn new things?

It's very important. You have to constantly have your ear to the ground to see what's going on.

What sort of benefits do you get from trying out different positions?
I feel like I have to know how to do every job in the company because I'm CEO. Sometimes you are pitching for cash, sometimes you're sweeping the floor, and sometimes you are just making sure the lights are turned off. I think it's something like that when you run any sort of company whether it is a restaurant or a Web company.

Mona Lisa Wallace is Co-Founder and CEO of RealEco.com, an e-commerce company that aggregates thousands of eco-friendly business supplies. Before founding RealEco.com in 1998, Mona Lisa practiced law, providing legal representation and litigation support to responsible businesses, non-profits, and individuals including environmental companies and women on welfare. In addition to her law practice, she co-founded FindIt.Org, a Web-based non-profit providing online consulting, database access, and networking opportunities to other non-profit corporations. Mona Lisa is actively involved in the community, working directly with organizations including the American Civil Liberties Union, the San Francisco National Organization for Women and Bay Area Lawyers for Individual Freedom. As a practicing Buddhist, Mona Lisa balances her professional life with yoga, meditation, and a love for the outdoors.

EMILY HOFSTETTER
Experiment With Different Things
SiliconSalley.com
CEO

Tell me about your background and how you ended up where you are today.

My background is actually as a writer and a chef. I was a screenwriter, but I graduated from college with a degree in women's studies where I helped set up a model for women's healthcare in the SUNY system. I got out of school and became a chef in lower Manhattan and then got involved in screenwriting. I also wrote, recorded and produced three records with my band over the past couple of years that has really opened up my writing and marketing skills. I sold a screenplay in '93 to Disney/Touchstone. I created mostly as a chef for almost ten years, owning my own restaurant for two of those years. When the Web started showing itself I saw that as an opportunity once again to expand my writing and creativity in a more interactive medium. I met a group of tech people that shared my curiosities and passions. I saw that there was a need for content suppliers and people coming up with new ideas that would translate online, so I got involved with some Web developers, one being my business partner, Candice Nelms. I started writing as a freelancer, creating original content and writing proposals to bring in new clients for a Web development company in New York city around '97. Candice and I started working on some projects together and then we were brought on as a technical team for a startup ISP back in '98. We were given a large part of equity for that company and developed some of its technology. Unfortunately we were not happy working with them because it just didn't seem like a company that was moving fast enough for us, or in the right direction, at the time, so we dumped our equity and started SiliconSalley.com.

What do you enjoy most about what you're doing today?

The pace at which I'm allowed to work, because I can actually take the many ideas that I have and put them into action. I can send out an inquiry to somebody with an idea and within a couple of hours I can have a response from anywhere in the world. The next day we set the idea into motion and see it through. Trial and error combined with real faith and patience is how we keep it going on a day-to-day basis. You have to believe in what you are doing and you have to

109

have a commitment to be in it for the long haul. I enjoy the process. I am learning every day, breaking ground in an industry that is brand new. It's a great feeling to be on the inside, from the beginning, building from the ground up. Who knows where we will end up? I just know that I enjoy the challenge of watching it all happen.

What do you think are your best attributes that have helped you through your career?

Probably my ability to conceptualize and take something like technology and apply it in an interdisciplinary way because I have a background that comes from so many different facets. It's the ability to really draw from all my experiences and to apply them to something like technology and new media, which runs the gamut.

What has surprised you the most about your career as it has developed?

The fact that people call me and ask me for advice, when I've never really considered myself as necessarily a leader. But people are finding me, my partner and our intrinsic message inspiring. I guess that's what surprises me the most, that people are looking to me to help get them started. It's a great feeling.

What has been the best piece of business advice you've received along the way in your career?

That's easy, "Greed is not a branding strategy." That a good idea is a good idea and bad ideas will never make money. If you have a brand, then you will have something to work off, but just because you want to make a lot of money doesn't mean you're going to come up with a good idea. Therefore if I was in this game to get my piece of the Internet pie, then I better get out of it and just move on.

If you have a good idea like that how important do you think good management is? Can you have a good idea and poor management?

I don't think it's going to fly on the first attempt without the management - unless of course you are really well connected and really lucky. I think you definitely need all the components that go with the good or great idea, and we're kind of seeing that come down the pipe right now.

110

What is the best piece of personal advice you've received with respect to your career?

Personally, it's, "find out what you love to do and then figure out how to get paid for it and don't forget to have fun while you're doing it." I think it came about from doing things too often where I was just motivated to pay the rent. After a while you find out you've been doing something you're really not enjoying and it becomes a chore. A job doesn't have to be a chore.

What are the biggest issues that you've faced with respect to succeeding at a demanding job and also having a personal life?

That life is short and you shouldn't pass up a chance to do the things that you love to do with the people that you love, because they'll always be more work but there might not be an experience. I'm going through that now with my sister who just had a baby, and it's very important to stop working at least one day a week and go spend time with her, her husband and the baby because that's my family. That baby is never going to be 7 months old again. It's about finding the time to do the things you really love to do and then you'll find more enjoyment in your work.

How hard was that early on in your career?

Devastatingly hard, because you get so wrapped up in it. You just keep going round and round thinking, "Okay, I'll work really hard right now and down the road I'll be able to take time off." But it just snowballs. Sometime I wake up at two in the morning, four in the morning, and there's always something to do. I will always have work to do but if I have the opportunity to enjoy myself, I should take it.

How have you created balance in your personal life and your career?

I know that there are things that must be done. My head will not be clear to do productive work if I don't go to the gym when I should, so I go every day. It helps me think clearly, because one usually facilitates the other.

How important are setting goals, and how should you update them?

Setting goals is very important. It's as important as a business plan is for your business. It's a road map for you to follow, not just to have something to raise money or to show somebody you have a goal or a plan. It's for yourself and it's very important to update them just like you would backup your hard drive. Look at something and cross it off your list, and say, "There's an accomplishment, and that's great. I'm going to reward myself for it." Unless, of course, you're setting unrealistic goals. I think a lot of people do that too.

What types of goals did you set for yourself early in your career?

That I was never going to make a promise that I was never going to be able to keep, and that I was never going to put myself someplace that I was going to regret later on.

How important has the Internet economy been for providing opportunities for women?

I think it's been incredibly important. I don't know that it's the Internet economy, but rather the Internet as a communication medium. I think that it's been important in many ways, one being that it's brought us to a point where people are entering the skill set levels at the same point, so if a woman wanted to start learning say XML programming, these things are developing so quickly that a woman and a man can enter at the same position. On that point I think the Internet is very, very important for women, because it's developing at a pace where everyone's learning at the same curve. I also think that it's opening up areas for networking so that women can network and communicate with each other on a global level. Big picture thinking is essential.

Do you have any good examples of that?

If I have a project that I'm working on, maybe client services or development with my partner here in SiliconSalley.com, and we need somebody who has certain skills, perhaps in programming, that we don't have, we can contact somebody from our database who might live in France or in Italy or in the Midwest or something. If this woman has those skills, she can make money by doing that programming for us. It opens up opportunities for us to be in touch with talented people who we wouldn't ordinarily know because we weren't in the same location.

Last year $35 million in venture capital was invested in Internet companies but only 4 percent was allocated to women. Well, I think it's a pipeline issue. You also have to ask yourself the question, were only 4 percent of the people who applied for venture capital women? That's important too, because ordinarily women haven't felt like they've had the same opportunities as men. We haven't had entry to the same network that men have had. The people who were holding the cash weren't our buddies, so we just couldn't call them up and say, "I need $20 million." I think that women haven't been thinking that large in the past. Instead, you've seen a lot of micro-loans and a lot of smaller amounts going to women to start "small businesses." But I think that's really going to change now because women are thinking a lot bigger. However, I do think that we are apt to ask for less because we are not excessive - it has less to do with not thinking big and more to do with wanting to prove ourselves incrementally and build out for longevity.

Was it difficult for you to get capital when you started out?

We are a self-funded company, and client services that come out of SiliconSalley.com really pay for SiliconSalley.com the magazine. We haven't looked toward any funding. We haven't needed it yet, but the company's grown so fast that we're going to build it out, and we're going to be looking for funding very soon.

In the last couple of years has it become harder or easier for women as a group to advance in their careers?

It's sort of a mixed bag, and it will always be a mixed bag. I think certain things do hold women back and one of those things is the basic language that's used in business. I do think that it's getting a lot easier from my point of view only because I see how far I've come in just one year, and that has a lot to do with the type of business I'm running and the medium that I'm running it in.

Are there any other specific impediments that women must overcome in the industry?

I think the fact that the tech industry, new media and technology specifically has never really been seen as a woman's industry because they're not the kind of beings that have wanted to hunker down in cubicles and program for 30 hours at a time. But you're seeing that happen a little bit more, and I think what you're going to see is women at the helm of these companies. We're starting to be seen more in executive management, which is a great sign, a fantastic sign. I think there are impediments in every industry. If I had to pick the most heinous in this industry I would have to say good old fashioned sexism and sexual harassment - these Dot.coms should get together on the HR front. Just because you want to have free environment in the "loft/office" I think you need to be careful how you speak to some employees or how you "joke around" when you have one woman in the company and she becomes the "Mommy." That's always a problem - women being ushered into stereotypical roles in the workplace.

Did you ever have a mentor that helped direct you in your career?

Not one person specifically, no. I do look to people as advisers every single day, however. I firmly believe in mentors and role models. I think that they are essential. Hopefully that is one of the functions that SiliconSalley.com is serving as - a showcase for future role models.

How important has networking been in your career?

It's been incredibly important. I don't think it could really have been as effective if my partner and I had tried to do it without the Internet. There just aren't enough hours in the day to get to all of the events - besides, as women, we have much catching up to do in that arena - the Internet has allowed us to really take it on at warp speed.

Do you have any examples of that?

You can send out an email and most likely you'll get that person writing you back or their PR person. We're about to do an interview with Sally Ride, the first woman in outer space, and we were talking about how would we have gotten to Sally Ride if it wasn't through the friend of a friend of a friend, email leads to email. When SiliconSalley.com was first launched we found that profiling one woman led to five others. Now we're finding that profiling one woman is leading to 30, and that's how the network is building out. We're in 14 countries right now and if I don't know somebody, somebody else in my network does.

What advice would you give to a woman trying to succeed in the business world today?

Nothing's impossible. If you have a clear vision of what it is that you want to do and surround yourself with people who are like minded and willing to work as hard as you are, you'll probably achieve your goal if it is set in a realistic manner and you're doing it for the right reasons and your motivation is your passion that is driving you.

What have been some of the most difficult choices that you've had to make in your career, and how have you responded to them?

Not entering into certain partnerships with people just because they wanted to, doing what was right for the company and building it at a slower pace when you could just bust out and make a big hype statement. We did not want to go too fast.

What are the skills women should be learning right now in order to excel in the future?

How to be very comfortable and say what you want, how to articulate what it is that you're looking for and what your goals are and how to say, 'I need this.' Not to be afraid to say that either your vision or your idea is worth funding or listening to.

How should women acquire these skills? What helped you grow in this way?

To be able to speak up is just something that you have to learn how to do. It takes practice. Deciding what you're willing to accept and what you're not willing to accept, setting boundaries and limitations and working within the parameters that you find acceptable so that you get up every day and really do what you want.

How important are technology skills?

That depends to what degree you will be implementing technology both into your business and into your personal life. Will you need to have hands on knowledge? In my case and in regard to SiliconSalley.com they're extremely important. I don't mean to say that you need to become a C++ programmer overnight or something like that, but I think you need to know how to navigate and how to negotiate that space right now. Having a level of proficiency and command of technology will in the long run empower you as a leader and save you money.

What are some good resources for women to develop these skills?

I just think they need to get online. They need to read as much as they can in terms of newspapers and their industry magazines but take them with a grain of salt. I think that sometimes the 'Dummies' books are really good as a way of approaching it from a basic level. Look at what's available online such as organizations, like Linux Chicks. Through digital TV you can see programs like Tech TV that offer tutorials, and there are online educational programs specifically for women, like PallasLearning.com that comes out of Canada. If you invest some time in researching e-learning programs and online Universities you'll find there are some great tutorials as well as degree programs.

Do leaders have to make sacrifices to have a successful career? Are there any examples of sacrifices that you had to make?

Absolutely. I think you always have to make sacrifices, but they're not considered sacrifices once you start to reap the rewards. I don't think it's about being a leader or being a member of a team, it's just about learning lessons. Everybody has to make sacrifices. A year could go by and you lift your head up and you realize that you haven't had a personal life, or you can't go to every event, you can't go to every conference, maybe you'll have to miss out on taking a big bundle of money because you're not ready at the moment, but you have to remember that you have to sacrifice money sometimes in order to have a clearer vision. Nothing great ever came easy and revolutions don't just come walking down the middle of the street - at least they are not recognized by the masses when they do.

What do you feel women must do differently than men in order to succeed?

Absolutely nothing. I think you just have to have confidence. I don't think there's any distinction between gender when it comes to success.

Are there any specific opportunities that the Internet economy presents specifically to women?

I think we're on a pretty common entry level with men. It's all about the learning curve. You can accelerate at the pace you choose to, so if you really do get it in terms of learning, you can become a fast learner and position yourself as an early adopter. Then you can really make it. Just keep all of your options open and never kill an idea until you are sure it cannot bend.

What kind of advice would you give to a startup?

Once again, don't get involved with the idea of greed, and make sure that you have a vision of what it is you want to do and that you have your management in line. When you look at the new economy, what's really so new about it? A business is a business, and you're going to try to move toward profitability. That's your goal, to make money - otherwise, it's called a hobby or a past time. If you can't see the future, there probably isn't one.

What types of different skills do people need in technology companies as opposed to brick-and-mortar companies?

Across the board you're looking at traditional business skills. I don't think that there's one "Superman" skill that you need to do if you're going to go for a tech company. Business is business, and everybody should be well-rounded. I think people should read philosophy and they should know about history and literature. Just because you're working in a tech company doesn't mean that you need to go overboard on your tech knowledge. Stay alert and do your best to stay positive no matter what.

How do you overcome the endless road bumps and obstacles that it takes to become a leader?

I think you have to learn from your team. Sometimes you have to learn how to admit when somebody else has a really good idea. You need to sit back, listen, take a lot of things in, and not talk too quickly. You also have to have thick skin. People will talk about you - jealousy and envy are green monsters - stay away from them.

Do you feel that it's important to force yourself into new positions and new things?

I don't think forcing is ever good. You have to relax into learning things, and you have to be comfortable with who you are in order to learn, period. I do believe in taking risks, however. Very exciting. Very sexy.

What are the main things that impress you about the people you work with?

Their ease of transforming from one way of thinking to another. My partner can go from dealing with legal matters, contracts and financial stuff, to becoming very creative on a campaign or doing designs. When I see adaptability, creativity and innovation I know that I am working with the right people.

Being a leader, is it easier spending your career in one company or branching out into different companies?

I think you need to branch out into different areas of your life. You can't just be a leader by submerging yourself in the business world, or in corporate structure or in on facet of a company. Sometimes you learn by taking your dog out for a walk and talking to your neighbors. If you become too narrowly focused, you'll never be a great leader.

Is it different today than 20 years ago before we had the Internet economy?

In theory it's not any different. Experience has changed over the past 20 years, obviously, so there are many more opportunities, but you have to be careful where your information is coming from and make sure it's authenticated. The bottom line is that everything you do in your life will make you a better leader if you're just willing to become a great observer.

What do you feel are the three most important things it takes to succeed on both a personal and a business level going forward?

That's difficult to break it down into just three. I'd say creativity, assertiveness and humility, but patience as well, and probably a clear, open mind too. It's a recipe that far exceeds the three ingredients rule but still retains the individuality of all of its flavor components.

How does patience help you?

As our dear friend and adviser Bill Key once said, "If you're in a hurry to get up, you're going to hurry up and fall."

Emily is Co-Founder, President & CEO of Silicon Salley Inc., an Internet Company dedicated to promoting visibility and creating opportunities for women in technology and new media.

Emily began her career creating new high concept business models with an emphasis on original creative content in 1993 when she was invited to become a member of The Writer's Guild of America, East as a "hot property" screenwriter. Making her first deal at the young age of 26 with Touchstone/Disney, Emily proved herself a player in a fiercely competitive Industry where her talents to communicate and generate ideas quickly took her skills and level of thinking to a higher plateau.

Never content to rest on her laurels, Emily then tackled another creative and competitive Industry as chef/owner of her own NYC restaurant/café known as Henrietta's Feed and Grain located in Manhattan's West Village.

Post tenure as a local celebrity chef, Emily was recruited to replace Jeff Buckley as lead singer in the power trio "Gods and Monsters" where she successfully served as front woman for almost two years. In 1997 she left the band to take the helm and reinvented herself once more as Eudora, performing singer/songwriter, where she wrote, recorded and released 2 full length CDs.

Emily received her Bachelor's degree in Women Studies from SUNY Purchase (1988) where she concentrated on adapting women's literature for performance.

LISA HENDERSON
Do What You Enjoy
LevelEdge
Founder & CEO

Tell me a little bit about your background and how you ended up where you are today.

I actually started my career in Consumer Packaged Goods, so I have a very classic, big-brand marketing background. I started my career at Ralston Purina in St. Louis. After I spent about five years there I decided to live in a big city. My boss at Ralston Purina made the big mistake of sending me to sales training in San Francisco. I thought it was an incredible place and decided to relocate to San Francisco. So I then made the very bold move of leaving an extremely good job at Ralston Purina, where I had just completed a successful new product launch, and came out to San Francisco with my resume and luggage. I decided to just give it a go and find myself a job when I got here. I was fortunate enough that I landed a job at a package goods company called Harmony Foods in Santa Cruz. I consciously didn't want to go to any of the big package goods companies because I was looking for something more entrepreneurial, so I went to work for Harmony Foods, which was only $172 million in those days, which was very small compared to the $1 billion-plus Ralston Purina. I worked for Harmony Foods for a couple of years when a huge Japanese confectionery company acquired it. I left shortly thereafter and went to work for Del Monte. They actually ran products out of Mexico, so I was based in San Francisco but spent a lot of time in Mexico looking for import and export opportunities for their manufacturing facilities there. I then worked for Specialty Brands, another packaged goods company in San Francisco. I ran a $175 million brand portfolio and was on my way. They offered me the general manager job in Australia and some other very senior level positions. The next president of the company and I, however, decided that if I took either of those roles I would probably be in package goods forever. What I really wanted to do was try to get into technology. That was six years ago.

Nobody had made the change from package goods to technology, so everybody thought I was insane. A company was brave enough to bring me on, Autodesk, and the CEO, Carol Bartz, was bold enough to support my move. Although she has never told me this herself, Carol Bartz got my resume, through a mutual friend, reviewed it, made a few calls to people she knew, got great feedback, took my resume to an executive staff meeting and said, "Somebody needs to hire this person because I think she's got the kind of background we need to start looking for." As a result, I was hired into the advance products group.

At that time, our objective was to look for new opportunities for Autodesk technology. A product they were working on was taking the CAD design platform and reinventing it for the consumer space so consumers could redecorate and remodel their homes using software. We had this wild idea then that we should have something on the Internet that would allow consumers to buy wallpaper, paint, furniture and refrigerators online. This was aggressive and visionary at the time, considering there was no such thing as e-commerce. So we started with that vision, we worked on the project, and the software itself was very successful. Autodesk made the decision to move away from low-end products and focus on their high-end products and we spun that company off and sold it. The product we launched at Autodesk called Picture this Home evolved to GoodHome.com, so the vision was completely carried through all the way to the Internet to being a commerce site for home decorating and remodeling.

That was my introduction to the Internet. When we finished that project, I did a few more things for Autodesk and then told Carol that I was going to leave and look for opportunities to help Internet companies launch, which was a few years ago. I started a consulting company, and I was one of the original three people who worked on Lucy.com. Then I worked on HungryMinds.com, which was bought my IDG. Then I was brought back to Autodesk to help them spin out what is now Buzzsaw.com. With that Internet experience under my belt, I was ready to build LevelEdge.

What interested you about being in an entrepreneurial atmosphere after being in such a comfortable role at such a large company?

There are two ways to look at a role in a very large company. Comfortable is one, but the other way is to say, "This is getting me a lot of experience being involved with a very significant brand." What I always liked and looked for, even in large companies, were those opportunities to do something very entrepreneurial, to do something very different, to either grow that business organically or to bring in an entirely new franchise that could fit within their strategic umbrella. I found Autodesk to be an excellent environment. I went back to help them do Buzzsaw, and that opportunity just wasn't available while I was at Autodesk. I have always sought out the higher-risk and more entrepreneurial ventures in every company I've worked at. I've done 107 new product launches, so in every single company, in multiple industries, I have always found myself in the role of starting up new divisions or starting up new products. I'm beginning to wonder if it's something in my genetic makeup, that's really my calling and what I'm best at doing.

What do you think are your best skills that have enabled you to succeed in this area?

A couple of things. I have always been very interested in trends and behavior. I actually find it fun to anticipate where certain markets are going to move, specifically in the area of consumers and consumer products. I also love the analytical side of identifying what needs are not being met by a marketplace. I think it's just a gut feeling that I have. I continually come up with new ideas. I've named a number of products, and I have done the branding. I don't know if it's training or if it's just the instinct of identifying and coming up with ideas to fill a particular gap. I have done this for as long as I can remember. My mother tells me stories of when I was an athlete growing up and I was told by my soccer coach, who was my uncle, that if I was going to play with the boys (there was no girls team) that I would have to have much stronger legs. I was about 8 years old, so I kept thinking how I was going to get stronger legs. On a piece of paper I drew out how I was going to get stronger legs. I took bricks, the kinds that have the holes drilled in them, and I ran shoestrings through them, and I tied them to the bottom of my shoes and marched around the backyard. So I claim to have invented the very first ankle weights. I did not have the marketing savvy at 8 to put my bricks on the market, however. When I look back and I talk to my family, they tell me that I was taking everything apart and putting it back together, that I was adding this to that to make it something else, and that I basically drove everyone crazy. Now they pay me to do it, so I guess it's a good thing.

How did seeing a couple of different industries help you decide what you wanted from your career?

I had worked in a very sophisticated and mature industry. Consumer package goods have been getting people to buy things for a very long time, and it has always been a very consumer-driven business. Therefore, the majority of the decisions were made around your knowledge of how consumers behave, their buying patterns and how can we get them to use more products. When I went into technology, everything was purely technology driven. I remember in my interview process with the CTO, he said two things to me. He said, "First of all, the way we launch technology products is completely different than the way you launch consumer products," and I said, "Let me give you my understanding of how a technology product is launched." I had done a flow chart without a title, diagramming all the critical steps. I asked, "Is this how it's done?" He looked at me and said, "Yes, that's pretty close." I responded by telling him that this was exactly how I have approached consumer products. I said the only thing that's distinctive here is I spent a little bit more time up front finding out what people really want versus identifying what cool features I can put in it. I was able to take 10 years of learning from package goods folks and use the pieces that were relevant to technology. So I think that had I just been a pure technologist, I would approach things purely from functionality and a technology perspective. Having the discipline from being in a consumer-driven and marketing-driven organization and going to technology at a time when it was neither of those things was extremely valuable.

What has surprised you the most over your career?

What was most surprising to me was the foundation around the Internet, and in its beginning, the lack of interest around its financial aspects. I came from an environment where I was paid on an operating profit. I was paid to drive and achieve certain revenue and market share goals. I was responsible for every line on the income statement and on the balance sheet that related to my brand. I can remember when I first planned for LevelEdge, I spent an unbelievable amount of time building a financial model, and very few people looked at it. That was the first thing that I found a little bit unnerving about the process. I had to, at that point, retrain my brain to think only about market potential and not so much how we were going to turn that into revenue. That was surprising and a discipline change for me. What is now interesting is that one of the most important things on my resume is that I run profitable businesses that CEOs or potential investors have all heard of.

The other thing that I found surprising is there are very few women in the organization. To go from package goods, which has a lot of women employed at all levels, into the technology industry is a very dramatic change. There were not many women in this industry. Even at a company like Autodesk that has a woman CEO, it was still challenging to bring in a lot of women. In those days it had a lot to do with the technology curve in a profession primarily of men. I was at a package goods environment where they had lots of men, lots of women, and the primary target audience was females. I can remember I joined a woman's management group at Autodesk. Autodesk has a couple thousand employees. There were about 40 women who belonged to that group. I thought that if we had this at Purina, there were 200 people just in the marketing group alone. So it was a big surprise. I got into a conversation with a woman at International Management Group, and I told her about it. She suggested that I talk to Billie

Jean King and arranged for the phone call. I told Billie Jean about my women's management group, and it ended with her telling me to let her know if I want her to speak to my group. I thought that would be incredible. A few weeks go by, my phone rings, and my assistant tells me that Billie Jean King is on the line. I about fell out of my chair. Billie Jean told me that she was coming out to do a charity event in San Francisco and that she was staying with her friend in Sausalito. She asked if I wanted her to come up and meet with the women of Autodesk. Billie Jean attended, and from that point on we probably had about 80 women attend our managers group. When she came out, she spent two hours telling the group about her personal experience with breaking a mold. It was an incredible transformation of that group and a tremendous transfer of confidence. It was one of those moments where you realized that women breaking into technology in those days were really doing just that, breaking into something. It was a terrific experience.

How important is it for women to have role models?

I think it is very important. Just about everyone I have talked to and told that story to has told me similar stories. This figure does not have to be someone of celebrity status, it can be a very good boss, for example. Probably the most important thing is recognizing that people are making those types of contributions to you. A lot of people, if you ask them to sit down and really think about it, don't realize there were these three or four people along the way who really influenced them and helped to shape their style of management and their approach to business. I think it is important to draw on the experience of others and learn how to motivate yourself to high levels from their examples. I have never met anyone who said that there was no one who had ever inspired them.

With so many new opportunities and companies emerging, have business cultures been redefined?

Absolutely. This is not a new phenomenon that technology went through. The auto industry went through it. They finally realized that women buy cars too. I think every industry has evolved to include more cultures. Now, more and more it doesn't matter whether you are a man or woman. I think that evolution comes naturally, but the fortunate thing in technology is that everything evolved so quickly that there was a very short window of time where we saw more women and minorities starting to get into the industry as well. So I think it's something that we've seen evolve on a much rapid curve than it did in other industries which is very, very positive.

What are some of the best pieces of advice you have received from a business standpoint along the way in your career?

My first boss, the guy who took a chance on hiring me at Ralston Purina, gave me some very good advice. Growing up I used to drive by the checkerboard and I knew they did a lot with pets so I earmarked them as a place I was going to work when I was about 12. I went to him and talked to his assistant and she told me they had no positions and that he could not talk to me. I got the standard blow off, but finally I convinced him to just take three minutes and just talk to me on the phone. He agreed and gave me an informational interview. At the end of the interview he said, "I'm not one to sit here and advocate that you just keep pounding a door, especially if people keep closing it on you, but the fire with which you've done it has always left a little bit of that door open, and I'm going to help you out. We don't have a job, but I'm going help you because I just like the way you've approached trying to create an opportunity here." I kept giving him ideas and I told him that I would be happy to just do project work and that he didn't even have to pay me. I just wanted any way to get my foot in the door. He got me interviews with Anheuser Busch and another big market research firm that they used as a supplier of information, and both places came back and said were going to make me a job offer. He called me at home and said I was going to get job offers from both of these places and he asked me not to take them, but he couldn't tell me why. I thought to myself, you have got to be kidding, I'm making about $10,000 a year, and I shouldn't take this job. A week later he called me and hired me as a senior research analyst and paid me $24,000. I almost died. He told me that when I was continually trying to identify a window of opportunity where I could get in and prove myself, I got him thinking about what his company could do with someone like me. He told me that I really need to make sure that I apply that technique in everything I do and to always look for a little bit different angle in which to approach things.

I've had a lot of good advice as the years have progressed. Another significant piece of advice was from Carol Bartz when I got into technology. She told me her story and rise to being the CEO of Autodesk and I found it very inspirational. She told me that it is sometimes going to be impossible to move the mountain, so you have to go over or around it to get where you need to be. She was one of the first women to get a computer science degree and her background is just phenomenal. I have often thought about the mountain that I have to move and finding other ways to navigate around it.

How have you found a balance between managing your business and your personal life?

While at Specialty Brands my boss and I worked ungodly hours. We turned on the lights in the office and locked the door at night. I ran the whole new products group. Basically it was a two-person team when I started and we developed 26 new products in six months. He called me in one day, and he said, "I want to understand how exactly you do this. You work these incredible hours and everyday you come in and check on me to see if I need anything. You're the open-door senior manager who everyone goes to for advice. How is it possible that you do this?" I said, "First of all, you have to have a passion and love what you do. If you don't, it will create tremendous conflict, so I wake up every day and I love being here and I love what I do. It's how I'm choosing to spend my time, but I also know when I have had enough and need to take that same energy and time and spend it on things from a personal perspective."

I think it's all about what you're passionate about and what you feel good about. Also recognize when you need to spend time on the personal things as well. I've been able to have a really good balance, mostly because I know myself really well. I know how far and how hard I can push and at what point I need to take time and get in touch with the personal things. Carol Bartz once said to me, "One of the things that I really admire about you is that you know yourself better than most people ever know themselves in a lifetime, so if you're telling me you need a new challenge or if this is what you want to do or this is how you're feeling, I can't say anything to that because I know you've thought about it and it's exactly what you want to be doing." So I think part of it is not losing sight that there are multiple facets to our lives, and that in the end, pursuing only one of them will not necessarily make you happy.

What do you find are the biggest issues women face with respect to succeeding at work and also having an enjoyable personal life?

I think we all face those challenges. I think the expectation for women, especially if there are children involved, is that they have to be much better at it. The reality is that if you have people who are important in your life, whether they're children, or spouses, or partners, you have to find a way to create that delicate balance that works for everybody involved. I know a number of women who are CEOs who are doing all of those things, and for them actually it's quite effortless. They're like, "Of course I have kids and of course I run my own company," and for others it is a struggle. I think it's not dissimilar from men who I've worked with. There was a gentleman I worked with in packaged goods who was about to have his third child and he said, "I feel like I've missed the first two's first five years. I'm not going to do it again." So I think the struggle exists whether you're male or female. I just think the expectation around women is that they're the ones who are going to make the stretch for family, especially if children are involved. I see women do it every day and it is remarkable, but I also think it's just something people do so that they can keep a balance and keep it all together.

You've always known what you wanted and what makes you happy, and I'm sure that didn't just come to you in your sleep, you thought about it and planned it out. How important are goals, how often should you revisit them and what should they cover?

I think they're extremely important. Every time I talk about my resume, my first impression is that I'm telling them about a lot of different places and different things I did. When I reflect back, that was by design. Every job that I've taken was because it was going to give me some new learning that I didn't have from the previous job, all with the eye on the ball of having my own company some day. A lot of people say that, but I grew up in a self-employed environment. My family owned a gas station. I worked there since I was 9 years old, and I decided that I wanted to own my own business for two reasons. The first was it was pretty cool that we went to this place and everybody knew that we owned it, and that was a fun thing. The second thing that I found and that put me over the top was I had the job of handing out paychecks. I was an extremely well liked young girl, everyone was just so happy to see me. I thought, "This is what I want to do for a living." So it was those experiences and the things I learned being in a self-employed family that made me think this would be a great thing to do.

I had to revisit the idea of starting my own company every time I got far along in an organization. At Ralston Purina I was the rising star. I'd won a number of marketing awards, everybody wanted me to work in their group, I was doing new products corporate wide. At Harmony Foods the same thing happened. At Specialty Brands I had taken on a huge international component, and they wanted me to move to the parent company in Australia. So every time there was a huge opportunity ahead of me, a huge title and usually huge dollars associated with it, I would ask myself, "Is that going to get me closer to doing my own thing?" My final test before I started LevelEdge, which was probably the toughest, was interviewing for a job at Hewlett Packard. They had offered the position to me and I had turned it down four times and they came back to me four times, so you can imagine how nice the offer was. It was right as I had just finished my business plan for LevelEdge. I've always been a fan of HP, and it was a very entrepreneurial organization, and Carly had just signed on. I knew all these things were very exciting, and it was significantly more money than I was making and I had to say no, because for me I was delaying myself, possibly pushing myself out of the market. If I had taken that opportunity, I'd still be at HP and I'd be thinking to myself, "I can't believe I didn't do the entrepreneurial thing and now the venture capital market is shrinking so now I really can't do it." I really struggled because it was the perfect position and in an interesting company, and I had to say no the fifth time and start a company I didn't even have any money to start. That was a pretty interesting crossroads. You have to test your commitment to those goals every time, and if your commitment changes or if there are other reasons or the goals evolve, that's perfectly fine, but recognize when something is taking you off track or really testing your commitment. I've made those decisions to either stay on track or to take a step to the left for a little while for whatever reason, but I am constantly in review. I don't think the goals would get better or challenging if you weren't constantly reviewing them.

Now that you've reached your goal of starting your own business, what are you enjoying most about it?

It's being able to put together what I consider a dream team of people. Some people are coming back and working for me a second and third time. I kept a notebook for 15 years of people who impressed me along the way, people who worked for me and people who in some cases I just came in contact with. I wrote down their names and their phone numbers and a little blurb about what impressed me, and I went through that notebook and started hiring those folks once I got funded. The most fun for me is that not only have I been able to put a great team of people together, but I've been able to get people to work for me repeatedly, which I'm hoping is an indication that I'm a good person to work for. It's an interesting environment. I get to work on something that's very meaningful to the marketplace that we're serving, and it's something I'm tremendously passionate about. When I followed those principles I've always made money, so my sense is that if you only stick your eye on the money ball it works for some people, but more often it doesn't work.

What do you think are the most important skills to have to succeed in business?

I think the most important skill often talked about that a lot of people don't have is good management skills. There is nothing that can compare to the ability to motivate people and the ability to share your passion and have people take it on as their passion. I've seen all kinds of management styles. I've seen what bad management and very egocentric management can do, and I've also had the

129

experience of working for very highly motivational good managers. Hands down, that guy (the highly motivational manager) wins every single time. Sometimes it takes him a little bit longer, but that individual always wins. I think that the trick is the ability to motivate people, articulate your vision and to have them buy into it and ultimately help you execute it.

What are some of the good resources for women, whether it's networking groups or mentors, to help them along in their careers?

I think we're getting more and more good organizations out there, and we're getting more and more women participating in them. There's the Women in Technology International, which puts on a lot of great conferences. Garage.com has done a great job of adding more and more women CEOs to its programs (they do a lot of CEO boot camps). I think the Forum for Women Entrepreneurs here in the Bay Area has done a tremendous job. They've put on the first ever women's venture capital forum, Springboard 2000. There are a number of organizations that are evolving and playing critical roles in supporting women entrepreneurs and CEOs.

What are the biggest challenges in terms of leading a company?

The biggest challenge is continually communicating your company's position and its distinctive role in the marketplace. Right now everything that has a Dot.com associated with it is getting lumped into one bucket. One of the challenges is to keep your company on the forefront, to continue to distinguish yourself versus other companies that are not in your space. The market tends to swing like a pendulum, where if you have a Dot.com in your name now, it's like a big black mark. You have to keep your employees motivated and engaged despite how the market is whirling around us. You have to create some stability in the environment. It's a constant job because all these variables around you are going to continually change and to keep your company evolving and moving in a direction that it can be successful is a daily challenge. You really have to stay on top of it.

How important is it to force yourself to learn new things every day?

That's actually the kind of environment that I thrive in. It's when I sit down and I realize that I've done everything that I can do inside of an organization or with a particular business that I've walked into my bosses and said, "I really feel like you're paying me too much for what I'm doing, because when you first brought me here I was doing this and this, and now it's kind of winding along and I've got 22 people reporting to me, which I really appreciate and I love, but I'm ready for someone else to do it, and I'm going to go on and do something else."

Tell me a little about what impresses you with respect to other people.

There are a number of characteristics. You can't have an organization of people just like me. It would be dangerous actually. I often respond to people who have better skill sets than me in a fixed area or bring a perspective to a business or a situation that I haven't seen or haven't been able to bring. I'm continually looking for not that perfect balance but for those people who will shake it up a little bit, people who are great implementers, people who are great visionaries and getting the right combination. It's like your stock portfolio. You're not going to go and put it all in a series of startups. You're going to put it into a balance of things so that at the end of the day your portfolio has the best potential for high performance. For me and those people who appeared in my notebook over the past 15 years, it could have been their overall presence, the way they communicated, the way they made eye contact, the way they engaged people in a conversation, all the way to people who are phenomenal implementers. As I started to build the company, I realized we need different skill sets in different areas, and you need different skill sets at different stages of the company as well. When you start a company you wear every single hat. I was the CTO, the CFO, the CMO. I was everything, and I can tell you I'm not good at that. I'm good at it for a period of time, but at some point there has to be someone in the organization that knows the technology 100 times better than I do and can manage and motivate an engineering staff. You have to recognize when and where you need to bring in those folks, and then hopefully you bring in the right kind of folks.

You've moved around quite a bit in your career and in different industries. Do you find it easier to get into a managerial position by moving around from company to company, or is it really more dependent on what you do?

When I made the move from packaged goods to technology, it was a demotion and $50,000 cut in pay, so I've always looked at the move from what kind of experience I am going to gain and what's the longer term implication of the move versus saying, "Oh, I need to move from company to company because that's how I'm going to get promoted." I was usually walking away from promotion opportunities to take another position that I thought had more opportunity to do something that I wanted to do. I never took a position as a title thing. In fact, twice I took demotions to get into organizations that I thought either had great growth potential or the opportunity was substantial or it was an industry change. But twice I've done it for the experience and to grow my portfolio out of being in one particular industry. So I look at those as short-term investments. I've always said, until recently, that I was just doing my own Ph.D.

It's actually worked to my advantage, but there's a point in time, especially in the consumer package goods area, where it wasn't looked upon favorably. There are people who have been in the same place for five or seven or 10 years, and I many times have had to explain when I made my move from package goods exactly what I just told you. I was always able to get really great jobs and do really well, but the industry didn't embrace that kind of behavior, and then I got into technology. Those guys were around a year and off to another opportunity or another interesting technology product to build, and nobody really cared if they came in and added tremendous value. They would have loved to have you for five years, but the expectation was you were only going to be there a couple. So that was a shift for me.

What advice would you give to other women trying to succeed in the business world?

Had the entire environment been a little bit different, I would have pushed earlier to take some of the risks and to get to a position where I was doing my own company. When I was building out my resume, I really thought it was important to have a vast amount of experience to give people. My advice is to determine what it is that you want to achieve and then make the decisions and the moves and whatever you need to do to get there sooner. I would have loved to do this five years ago, for lots of reasons. You only start your first company once, and knowing what I know, I would have loved to do it sooner. It's such a great experience. Don't be shy about going out and making it happen for yourself as soon as you can.

Would you recommend to other women to start their own business, and who are the best suited to do that?

Based on my experience, I would recommend that everybody have the opportunity to do this. It is truly incredible to bring an organization of people together and to see an idea that you have evolve 100 percent from the inside. But in this particular environment, you cannot be risk adverse. It's an extremely high-risk proposition, and it can also be extremely demanding. You are the business, every minute of every day. I can be out personally doing something and someone will have read an article on our company and want to talk to me that second. I could choose to say, "I'm not in the mood," or I can put on my corporate hat and talk about the company one more time. So it's very, very demanding and it's a very high-risk proposition, and you need to understand those two elements. And at the end of it I feel there's no losing scenario. I'll have had the most phenomenal experience no matter what happens, and you can't buy this kind of experience. But I think you've got to have a pretty good stomach to do it.

How important is it to enjoy what you're doing, and when you do enjoy it, what does it enable you to do?

If you do what you love, the fact that it's risky and it's very, very demanding, is something that you can go with because you're so passionate about what you're doing. If you're not passionate about what you're doing, you'll be in constant conflict, thinking, "I should be doing something else, or I don't really want to take that risk, I'm not that into it anyway." You'll find yourself in tremendous conflict either personally or professionally with how you're spending your time. That's what happened to me. As I moved through various companies I may have gotten to very high positions that everyone looked at and said, "Wow, that's really a phenomenal position." But I didn't wake up in the morning with that same passion. I've seen it happen with other people, and it affects how you feel personally and what you're able to contribute. I think having your passion at the core is what keeps you in the game from a healthy and a duration standpoint.

Lisa Henderson is the CEO of LevelEdge and responsible for management, market promotion and fund-raising. Prior to founding LevelEdge, Henderson managed the advertising, marketing and public relations activities as Vice President of Marketing at HungryMinds.com. She has consulted with several additional dot com companies and helped launch Autodesk, Inc.'s first Internet business, buzzsaw.com. Previously, Henderson held the Director of Marketing position for Autodesk's Personal Solutions Group, the first consumer division at the company. She has extensive experience in brand management and marketing, having managed over 100 products in three categories, including consumer goods and services, over the past 14 years. Henderson has held several senior management positions in both technology and consumer packaged goods, and her experience includes full-line business management and organizational responsibility ranging from startup to $175 million in revenue. She sits on the boards of directors for a non-profit organization, SportsBridge, and for two Internet startup companies. She holds an MBA in Finance and Marketing from Lindenwood University, where she was a scholarship athlete in basketball, soccer and softball as an undergraduate.

Business Intelligence Publications & Services

The C-Level Library ™

The C-Level Library enables you and your team to quickly get up to speed on a topic, understand the issues that drive an industry, identify new business opportunities, and profit from the knowledge of the world's leading executives. Thousands of books, briefs, reports and essays are broken down and organized by Aspatore Business Editors in a user-friendly format to ensure easy maneuvering and efficient researching. In just 10 minutes, you can be up to speed on any topic, or lay the groundwork to research any industry or job in The C-Level Library. Aspatore annually publishes C-Level executives from over half the Global 500, the top 250 professional services firms, the fastest-growing 250 private companies, MP/Chairs from over half the 250 largest law firms and leading executives representing nearly every industry. Content is updated weekly and available for use in various formats - as-is online, printed, copied and pasted into a PDA, and even emailed directly to you. Speak intelligently with anyone, on any topic or industry. Subscribe to The C-Level Library.

License/Bulk Orders of Content Published by Aspatore

For information on bulk purchases/licensing content published by Aspatore for a web site, corporate intranet, extranet, newsletter, direct mail, book or in another format, please email store@aspatore.com. For orders over 100 books/chapter excerpts, company logos and additional text can be added to the book.

Corporate Publishing Group (An Aspatore Owned Company)

Corporate Publishing Group (CPG) provides companies with on-demand writing and editing resources from the world's best writing teams. Our clients come to CPG for the writing and editing of books, reports, speeches, company brochures, press releases, product literature, web site copy and other publications. This enables companies to save time and money, reduce headcount, and ensure polished and articulate written pieces. Each client is assigned a CPG team devoted to their company, which works on their projects throughout the course of a year on an as-needed basis and helps generate new written documents, review and edit documents already written, and provide an outside perspective before a document "goes public" in order to help companies maintain a polished image both internally and externally. Clients have included companies in all industries and disciplines, ranging from financial to technology to law firms, and are represented by over half of the Fortune 500. For more information please e-mail rpollock@corporateapublishinggroup.com or visit www.CorporatePublishingGroup.com.

SmartPacks ™ — Get up to Speed Fast!

SmartPacks help you determine what to read so that you can get up to speed on a new topic fast, with the right books, magazines, web sites, and other publications (from every major publisher in the world including over 30,000 sources). The 2-step process involves an approximately 15 minute phone call and then a report written by Aspatore Business Editors and mailed (or emailed) to you the following day (rush options available).

Aspatore C-Level Research ™

Aspatore Business Editors are available to help individuals, companies, and professionals in any industry perform research on a given topic on either a one-time or a consistent monthly basis. Aspatore Business Editors, with their deep industry expertise at getting access to the right information across every medium, can serve as an external librarian/researcher for all your research needs.

Establish Your Own Business Library ™

Work with Aspatore editors to identify 50-5,000 individual books from all publishers, and purchase them at special rates for a corporate or personal library.

**To Order or For Customized Suggestions From an Aspatore Business Editor,
Please Call 1-866-Aspatore (277-2867) Or
Visit www.Aspatore.com**

Best Selling Books
(Also Available Individually At Your Local Bookstore)

REFERENCE

Business Travel Bible – Must Have Business Phone Numbers, Business Resources, Maps & Emergency Information

Business Grammar, Style & Usage – Rules for Articulate and Polished Business Writing and Speaking

ExecRecs – Executive Recommendations For The Best Products, Services & Intelligence Executives Use to Excel

The Executive Challenge – Business IQ & Personality Test for Professionals

The C-Level Career Guide – Find Out Which Industry and Career You Are Best Suited For

The Healthy Executive – 7 Ways For Business Professionals to Lead a Physically and Mentally Healthier Life

The Philanthropic Executive – Establishing a Charitable Plan for Professionals

The Business Translator-Business Words, Phrases & Pronunciation Guides in Over 65 Languages

MANAGEMENT/CONSULTING

Leading CEOs – CEOs Reveal the Secrets to Leadership & Profiting in Any Economy

Leading Consultants – Industry Leaders Share Their Knowledge on the Art of Consulting

Recession Profiteers – How to Profit in a Recession & Wipe Out the Competition

Managing & Profiting in a Down Economy – Leading CEOs Reveal the Secrets to Increased Profits and Success in a Turbulent Economy

Leading Women – What It Takes to Succeed & Have It All in the 21st Century

Become a CEO – The Golden Rules to Rising the Ranks of Leadership

Leading Deal Makers – Leveraging Your Position and the Art of Deal Making

The Art of Deal Making – The Secrets to the Deal Making Process

Empower Profits – The Secrets to Cutting Costs & Making Money in ANY Economy

Building an Empire – The 10 Most Important Concepts to Focus a Business on the Way to Dominating the Business World

Management Brainstormers – Question Blocks & Idea Worksheets

TECHNOLOGY

Leading CTOs – The Secrets to the Art, Science & Future of Technology

Software Product Management – Managing Software Development from Idea to Development to Marketing to Sales

The Telecommunications Industry – Leading CEOs Share Their Knowledge on The Future of the Telecommunications Industry

Know What the CTO Knows – The Tricks of the Trade and Ways for Anyone to Understand the Language of the Techies

Web 2.0 AC (After Crash) – The Resurgence of the Internet and Technology Economy

The Semiconductor Industry – Leading CEOs Share Their Knowledge on the Future of Semiconductors

Techie Talk – The Tricks of the Trade and Ways to Develop, Implement and Capitalize on the Best Technologies in the World

Technology Brainstormers – Question Blocks & Idea Development Worksheets

VENTURE CAPITAL/ENTREPRENEURIAL

Term Sheets & Valuations – A Detailed Look at the Intricacies of Term Sheets & Valuations

Deal Terms – The Finer Points of Deal Structures, Valuations, Term Sheets, Stock Options and Getting Deals Done

Leading Deal Makers – Leveraging Your Position and the Art of Deal Making

To Order or For Customized Suggestions From an Aspatore Business Editor,
Please Call 1-866-Aspatore (277-2867) Or
Visit www.Aspatore.com

The Art of Deal Making – The Secrets to the Deal Making Process
Hunting Venture Capital – Understanding the VC Process and Capturing an Investment
The Golden Rules of Venture Capitalists – Valuing Companies, Identifying Opportunities, Detecting Trends, Term Sheets and Valuations
Entrepreneurial Momentum – Gaining Traction for Businesses of All Sizes to Take the Step to the Next Level
The Entrepreneurial Problem Solver – Entrepreneurial Strategies for Identifying Opportunities in the Marketplace
Entrepreneurial Brainstormers – Question Blocks & Idea Development Worksheets

LEGAL

Privacy Matters – Leading Privacy Visionaries Share Their Knowledge on How Privacy on the Internet Will Affect Everyone
Leading Lawyers – Leading Managing Partners Reveal the Secrets to Professional and Personal Success as a Lawyer
The Innovative Lawyer – Leading Lawyers Share Their Knowledge on Using Innovation to Gain an Edge
Leading Labor Lawyers – Labor Chairs Reveal the Secrets to the Art & Science of Labor Law
Leading Litigators – Litigation Chairs Revel the Secrets to the Art & Science of Litigation
Leading IP Lawyers – IP Chairs Reveal the Secrets to the Art & Science of IP Law
Leading Patent Lawyers – The & Science of Patent Law
Leading Deal Makers – Leveraging Your Position and the Art of Deal Making
Legal Brainstormers – Question Blocks & Idea Development Worksheets

FINANCIAL

Textbook Finance – The Fundamentals We Should All Know (And Remember) About Finance
Know What the CFO Knows – Leading CFOs Reveal What the Rest of Us Should Know About the Financial Side of Companies
Leading Accountants – The Golden Rules of Accounting & the Future of the Accounting Industry and Profession
Leading Investment Bankers – Leading I-Bankers Reveal the Secrets to the Art & Science of Investment Banking
The Financial Services Industry – The Future of the Financial Services Industry & Professions
Empower Profits – The Secrets to Cutting Costs & Making Money in ANY Economy

MARKETING/ADVERTISING/PR

Leading Marketers – Leading Chief Marketing Officers Reveal the Secrets to Building a Billion Dollar Brand
Emphatic Marketing – Getting the World to Notice and Use Your Company
Leading Advertisers – Advertising CEOs Reveal the Tricks of the Advertising Profession
The Art of PR – Leading PR CEOs Reveal the Secrets to the Public Relations Profession
The Golden Rules of Marketing – Leading Marketers Reveal the Secrets to Marketing, Advertising and Building Successful Brands
PR Visionaries – PR CEOS Reveal the Golden Rules of PR
Textbook Marketing – The Fundamentals We Should All Know (And Remember) About Marketing
Know What the VP of Marketing Knows – What Everyone Should Know About Marketing, For the Rest of Us Not in Marketing
Marketing Brainstormers – Question Blocks & Idea Development Worksheets
Guerrilla Marketing – The Best of Guerrilla Marketing-Big Marketing Ideas For a Small Budget
The Art of Sales – The Secrets for Anyone to Become a Rainmaker and Why Everyone in a Company Should be a Salesperson

**To Order or For Customized Suggestions From an Aspatore Business Editor,
Please Call 1-866-Aspatore (277-2867) Or
Visit www.Aspatore.com**

ASPATORE

C-Level Business Intelligence™